The
Rock 'n'
Roll
Haggadah

T0349034

The Rock 'n' Roll Haggadah

Your Guide to a Seder That Rocks!

Meredith Ochs and Kay Miller

Simon Element

New York | London | Toronto | Sydney | New Delhi

**SIMON
ELEMENT**

An Imprint of Simon & Schuster, LLC
1230 Avenue of the Americas
New York, NY 10020

First Simon Element trade paperback edition March 2025

SIMON ELEMENT is a trademark of Simon & Schuster, LLC

For information about special discounts for bulk purchases, please contact Simon &
Schuster Special Sales at 1-866-506-1949 or business@simonandschuster.com.

The Simon & Schuster Speakers Bureau can bring authors to your live event. For
more information or to book an event, contact the Simon & Schuster Speakers
Bureau at 1-866-248-3049 or visit our website at www.simonspeakers.com.

Interior design by Kristina Juodenas

Manufactured in China

1   3   5   7   9   10   8   6   4   2

Library of Congress Cataloging-in-Publication Data has been applied for.

ISBN 978-1-6680-4744-6
ISBN 978-1-6680-4745-3 (ebook)

For Lita and David Gottesman,
who built the foundation of my life
on love, humor, faith, and reason.

—MO

To Ozzy and Sharon Osbourne,
for speaking up.

—KM

Contents

The Rock 'n' Roll Haggadah

foreword

Find the crack in the matzah.

It was the game my sister, Jude, and I played, savoring the overly sweetened Manischewitz, chanting the Four Questions, searching for the *afikomen*, singing the Pesach songs from "Dayenu" to the saga of the solitary kid that Father bought for Zuzim. *One kid, one kid.*

When you break a piece of matzah and then realign the pieces, it becomes seamless. You have to look carefully to see where it was wrought asunder. Within a parable about contemporary music embodying a tradition that goes back three and a third millennia, it allows us to see the past as it becomes the future.

Freedom, as much a beginning as an ending. The Passover tale, each plague dripping its blood into our remembrance, is not a merry stroll through forty years of desert after the parting of the Red Sea but a tale of continual, prayerful trial and tribulation and hopeful transcendence. The battles of bygone centuries are still within us, the chronicles of Nineveh and Jericho and the rivers of Babylon as alive today as in the Old Testament. We try to abide by those Ten rock-hewn Commandments, but the golden calf ever beckons with its gilt allure. The ritual unfolding of the Seder provides comfort, like singing along to a song you've heard many a time.

Why we sing. My chosen calling happens to be rock 'n' roll, both halves of that split in the matzah, hard to tell where the rock leaves off and the roll begins, its promise of liberation and illumination. I've spent a lifetime within its Psalms and Solomonic Songs, more than I've davened in shul; but then I've always aspired to be my own cantor, to recite the Torah of arcane artists and forgotten B-sides, amid all the ways humans express themselves in frequency response and rhythmic duration. To come into direct contact with the emotions of a ceremony that harmonizes our desire to be free, to divine our own judgment and path in life, and then perhaps, in contemplation, lean back and rest, for we are no longer slaves; to partake of the Passover plate, six stations of symbolism, surrounding the glass of wine awaiting the Prophet Elijah to take his sip.

It is my favorite moment of the Seder, after the home has been cleansed, the favored foods served—the gefilte fish, the lighter-than-air matzah balls, the chewy macaroon finale, though I'm sure that wasn't the chosen repast back in the shtetl.

I'm five, and it's my task to open the door for Elijah. I perform the sacred duty, to allow the divine presence entry into our home so he might lift a glass to the family within. When I open the door, there is my aunt Lillian preparing to knock. I knew then that she was an angel, sent to bless our home.

Another Passover, another family. I'm at Abbijane's Seder, along with some vets of the New York rock scene, remembering what it was like to be in the audience at a New York Dolls show. From the synagogue across from her back garden, the sounds of song vibrate the air, not quite heard but imbued with the familiar minor keys and lamentations and hallelujahs and supplications and always gratitudes, accompanying our prayers, the sacred spirit within us all.

Next year: in the Universe. And chorus.

Lenny Kaye
New York City
2024/5785

Introduction

When my friend Kay Miller asked if I'd like to collaborate on *The Rock 'n' Roll Haggadah*, I was ecstatic. I thought about my family's Seders and how many songs are interspersed throughout the evening as we go around the dining room table, reading passages on the exodus from Egypt. The rich aromas of Mom's brisket and tzimmes in the oven tormented us during the hour or more we spent on the weighty liturgical, historical, and philosophical matters leading up to the shulchan orech (the festive meal). Passover is one of the heavier and more complex Jewish holidays, in the classic mode of "They tried to kill us, we escaped, then we ate." To paraphrase the Who, Passover is meatier, beatier, bigger, and bouncier than other Jewish holidays because we're supposed to feel as if we ourselves "have gone forth from Egypt."

As my brother and I and our Seder-going friends got older, we began incorporating our own references into the story and the songs. We created instant mash-ups with bits of z'mirot (table songs), hymns we learned in shul, beatboxing that we learned in school, and rock, pop, punk, and reggae songs we loved. Recontextualizing the lore made us feel more connected to it, and the Seder is about connection—not only past to present but also with your family, friends, and far beyond.

That's why I loved Kay's idea of infusing a Haggadah with rock 'n' roll. Like the story of Passover, rock is rooted in oppression but is ultimately about freedom. There would be no rock music without blues, and there'd be no blues (nor jazz, hip-hop, R&B, or country) without African American field hollers and gospel. This, too, was part of the discourse at our family table. We started to take a broader historical view of tyranny and appropriation. We even churned over possibilities for peace in

the Middle East as each Seder ended with the chimera "Next year in Jerusalem." These things seem possible over copious amounts of wine, brisket, and song. So, feel free to deliberate and discuss whatever moves you at your Seder. Or just bang your head to the tunes.

As rock 'n' roll is the theme here, we intended for our book to be light of heart, but we take the holiday seriously. My parents saw to it that I never missed a Seder, a tradition my brother and I have continued as adults. When my dad was in the hospital with a terminal illness, we brought the Seder to him. During the COVID-19 pandemic, we helped my mom figure out Zoom so she could partake in our extended family's virtual Seder.

Historically, Jews have gone to extraordinary lengths to observe Passover. Seders have been held all over the world for thousands of years, in countries that were hostile to us, during wartime, even during the Holocaust. And although it's a Jewish holiday, it's fundamentally about universal human rights. Liberty, freedom of worship, the right to hold our leaders accountable—these are things that people are still being killed for, things we can never take for granted. For me, Passover serves as a reminder of the liberties

On his record *Exodus*, reggae icon Bob Marley drew from biblical stories, political unrest in Jamaica, and his escape to London after surviving an assassination attempt. *Time* magazine named it "Best Album of the Twentieth Century."

I've enjoyed as an American citizen. It reminds me of my luck that my ancestors escaped being murdered for the crime of being Jewish in central and eastern Europe. They arrived here as "strangers in a strange land" (my great-grandma, who already had kids of her own, attended kindergarten classes to learn English), where their roots grew into a family of doctors, lawyers, soldiers, teachers, writers, and more.

Whether you're a true believer who takes the fantastic story of the exodus literally, or you're a skeptic who believes only the scientific evidence that aligns with some of it, I hope you'll find meaning and entertainment in our Haggadah. Even if you doubt the miracles described ahead, consider the miracle that the Jewish people have managed to survive and thrive for thousands of years, despite relentless attempts to annihilate us. Our very existence is an astonishing tale, making the Passover Seder and its narrative arc of oppression and emancipation ever relevant.

While growing up in London, singer Amy Winehouse honed her vocals on Jewish hymns her parents taught her. She and producer Mark Ronson bonded over their shared Jewish identity.

—Meredith Ochs

A few Notes About This Haggadah

The Rock 'n' Roll Haggadah is unique. Standard Haggadahs tend to start abruptly, diving right into the formalities. We wanted ours to be expansive, a helpful guide for those celebrating Passover or hosting a Seder for the first time, an alternate approach for those looking to make their Seders more fun and inclusive, and a deeper dive into storytelling. Unlike most Haggadahs, ours begins with a section on preparing for the holiday and some of the lore involved, and our Seder itself includes more fascinating stories about the exodus, both biblical and historical. It's a book you won't want to file away after Pesach, but it's also a real Haggadah with rituals and brachot (blessings). The sidebars about our "Honorable Menschen" bring additional knowledge and pop culture curios. Add whatever you'd like to elaborate on the basic observance in a way that is relevant to you and your guests.

Throughout the text, we've included song titles that tie into the narrative and/or Jewish traditions in one way or another. You'll find these songs in the *Rock 'n' Roll Haggadah* playlist at the end of the book, as well as our Spotify playlist of the same name. The songs are meant to spark inspiration as you prepare for the holiday and conversation at the table, or to be played at the table if you desire. For some observant Jews, singing and dancing at the Seder are customary; if you're moved to borrow from that tradition, go for it. Passover has many practices built into the holiday to teach children and keep them engaged during the Seder, and this is another way to do that. If there are kids attending, put them in charge of playing the music at the appointed times; they're probably the most technologically inclined people in the house anyway. We've added a visual key near certain songs—a treble clef 𝄞—to serve as a prompt, as well as highlighted other songs mentioned in the book, but play or sing or discuss as you wish.

Like many texts, we use the words "Israelites," "Jews," and "Hebrews" interchangeably, as well as "Israel," "Canaan," and "the Promised Land." Technically, Jewish people in Egypt (also called Mitzrayim, derived from the word for narrow straits or a narrow place) were Israelites. It wasn't until after we left that we received the Torah, the books containing the basis of our laws and teachings. The land of Israel, where we'd lived pre and post our sojourn in Egypt, was called Canaan. It has been fought over and vanquished by empires and called other names between then and now.

We also make reference to God (Hashem, Adonai or Adonoi, Ruler or Sovereign of the Universe), the monotheistic, incorporeal Jewish deity. This doesn't mean you must be devout, or even Jewish, to participate in the Seder. Part of the Seder—the Four Children—addresses varying levels of spiritual belief, including zero belief. Yes, this is a religious event, but it's also about family, community, and tradition . . . plus food, wine, and music. We cover a lot of ground in this book with one fundamental missive: All are welcome.

Absolute Beginners:
A Passover Newbie's Guide

A full Moon festival

Unlike the Gregorian calendar, by which most of us schedule our lives, the Hebrew calendar is lunisolar. That's why Jewish holidays fall on different dates from year to year, and that practice began with Passover.

In the Book of Exodus, just before the Tenth Plague is to be visited upon the Egyptians, God commands the soon-to-be-freed Israelites to start keeping a calendar based on the moon. It's the first thing we're told to do, as free people are in charge of their own time. It marks the departure from Egypt, a sun-worshipping, intransigent culture gripped by a caste system, both physically and ideologically. We were about to become **"One Nation Under a Groove,"** ♪ independent, governed by a set of laws rather than a king, answering to one God.

Like Tom Petty going solo, Jewish people have had *Full Moon Fever* ever since. Our holy days commence at sundown. We celebrate the new moon each month with Rosh Chodesh, a holiday some say was created for the Jewish women at Mount Sinai who didn't participate in the golden calf desert debacle (more on this later). Several of our holidays fall on the full moon, beginning with Passover, which is on the 15th of Nisan.

This is the date on which Pharaoh finally kicked us to the curb (though he soon changed his mind). It's the first full moon of Aries, a fire sign (fire is a motif throughout the Haggadah, as well as in rock 'n' roll) and a ram worshipped as a god by Egyptians. With Aries at its most ascendant, it's a date on which Pharaoh would have believed he'd be at the height of his powers, yet he was **"King Midas in Reverse."** ♪

Setting our holy days by the moon is also the reason Jews hold two Seders instead of one. That's right: after a long, wine-filled night of complex rituals, we don't sleep it off. Like Billy Preston, we do **"The Same Thing Again"** the following night. The tradition goes back to ancient Israel, when rabbis would certify the beginning of each month after two witnesses reported seeing the new moon. Messengers spread word throughout the land, but for Jews living outside Israel the delay was confusing, as they were uncertain which day to officially celebrate on. So, a yom tov sheni shel galuyot—a second Diaspora festival day—was declared. Within Israel, only one Seder is still the norm. Observant Jews celebrate Passover for eight days, the first two and last two of which are holy and filled with traditional practices and prayers. (In Israel, only the first and seventh days are considered holy.)

Tradition!

Explaining Judaism and our commandments (or mitzvot, though the word "mitzvah" is also slang for doing a good deed), customs, and practices makes us think of Avril Lavigne: it's **"Complicated."** There's the OG tome: the Torah, also known as the Five Books of Moses. Then there's the Talmud, which has two parts: the Mishnah, six books on Jewish law regarding everything from agriculture and settling civil disputes to how to comport ourselves in **"Houses of the Holy,"** 𝄞 and the Gemara, which is a discussion of the Mishnah, combining legal jargon with narrative—history, philosophy, folklore, and much more.

The extraordinary thing about these texts is that they set a precedent for the vigorous debate at the heart of Judaism. Minority viewpoints are valued and a winning side is not always clear, leaving much open to interpretation. This is one reason Jewish traditions vary so widely.

Another reason is also the reason the Talmud exists at all—persecution. This stuff was not originally meant to be written down. It was the "Oral Torah." After the destruction of both Holy Temples in Jerusalem, first by Babylonians (586 BCE), then by Romans (70 CE), and our expulsion from Israel, spiritual leaders figured that without a central governing body, it would be a good idea to start documenting their ways. Before Bob Dylan sang it, they could see that **"The Times They Are A-Changin'"** 𝄞 and would continue to do so. As Jews moved through the Diaspora for centuries, we adapted to make our traditions work within the structures of our adopted countries. In the Middle Ages, rabbis and scholars continued to discuss and progress Jewish thought and halacha ("the way"—i.e., Jewish law) that informs many customs we still keep, including much of what we do during the celebration of Passover. We evolved, so we survived.

Gene Simmons of KISS

He was born Chaim Witz and went by Gene Klein (his mother's maiden name) before choosing his stage name—inspired by rockabilly singer Jumpin' Gene Simmons and the 1964 hit "Haunted House." The song's farcical, schlock horror hinted at the New York rock band that Chaim would go on to found in 1973 with another nice Jewish boy, Stanley Eisen, aka Paul Stanley. The band, of course, is KISS.

Simmons was known to bring celebrity friends and flames to Passover Seders at the New York home of his mother, Florence, a Holocaust survivor. His guest list has included Diana Ross and her ex-husband Bob Ellis Silberstein (father of Tracee Ellis Ross), and Cher and her two kids. Even though Simmons would conduct the Seders, his mom freaked out a little at the prospect of his glamorous girlfriend (at the time) in her house. "I said, 'Gene, you're bringing Cher? She's such a fancy-schmancy lady,'" Florence recalled. "And Gene said, 'No, she's just an ordinary, nice person.' And Gene was right." In the tradition of welcoming anyone with nowhere else to go, Florence made sure Gene's chauffeur also had a seat at the Seder table. "I always invite him in," she said. "What's another plate?"

Seder Starter Kit

If this is your first rodeo, think of a Seder as a combination of ritual, reading, and dinner. Sure, you'll arrive at **"Meat City"** (respects to John Lennon) or its veggie equivalent eventually, but there are a few things you'll need for the rest of the festivities as well:

Go exponential on Emmylou Harris's "Two More Bottles of Wine." Each guest is supposed to drink four full glasses over the course of the evening and a series of brachot. If you keep kosher, you're inviting guests who do, or you're going to a kosher home for the Seder, make sure the bottles sport a kosher for Passover endorsement. Otherwise, drink what you like. Pro tip: get at least a magnum or two of Manischewitz or Kedem Concord Grape wine for sacramental and sentimental purposes.

A separate cup of wine for Elijah the Prophet. This will not be consumed by mere mortals.

A cup of water designated as Miriam's Cup to honor the women in the story.

Grape juice. This is for kids and teetotalers, so they can participate in the rituals as well.

Lots of matzah. For the Passover rituals, set three whole sheets of matzah on a separate plate and cover them with a large napkin or a designated cloth. Like all the ceremonial objects mentioned in this book, Judaica stores sell fancy Pesach matzah covers (some that will neatly tuck your stack of three into separate pockets) and trays if you want to be fancy; if you've inherited treasured ones from family, even better. Guess what—a regular plate and a large napkin works, too. You'll need an extra cloth in which to wrap the afikomen (the half piece you'll be hiding later). Keep more matzah on hand for folks to eat during the meal. If you're forgoing leavened foods for the entire holiday, you'll need enough to last your household a week.

KISS's "God Gave Rock and Roll to You II" is a remake of a song by the British band Argent.

Jack Antonoff's Jewish Perspective

A ten-time (and probably more by the time you read this) Grammy-winning musician, songwriter, and record producer, New Jersey native Jack Antonoff got his Hebrew education at the well-known private Solomon Schechter Day School. As a member of the band Fun, he made songs with soaring choruses and a dark underbelly, like their millennial anthem **"We Are Young,"** which won a Grammy for Song of the Year (2013), and **"Carry On,"** a paean to perseverance. Antonoff started the "side project" Bleachers in 2013, and he has collaborated with numerous pop stars, including Taylor Swift, one of his longtime besties, since her album *1989*.

Growing up with Judaism has been a plus in his life as a producer and music maker. "I think there's a Jewish perspective on life that's rather unique, which I find fairly beautiful and some people find completely annoying," he says. "It's like a built-in skepticism. I'm also looking at scenarios from just about every angle and sometimes thinking about how things could go wrong."

Scallions—optional. Persian and Afghan Jews have a fun tradition of swatting at each other with scallions while singing "Dayenu." To participate, make sure there are enough **"Farm Fresh Onions"** 🎵 for every guest.

In addition to your regular place settings, you'll want **supplementary small plates** if you'll be serving gefilte fish, small bowls (for salt water and egg), and soup bowls (matzah balls!) for each guest, plus additional bowls for serving charoset and spilling wine during the reading of the Ten Plagues (more on this later).

"Salt Water." Far less complicated than Ed Sheeran's: mix a spoonful of salt into each cup of water and stir. It doesn't have to be as salty as **"The Ocean"** 𝄞 (though that Led Zeppelin song does mention sitting around and singing all night, which we'll be doing), more like Smokey Robinson and the Miracles' **"Tracks of My Tears"** 𝄞—just enough to taste the salt.

Hard-boiled eggs. It's customary to serve an egg to each guest in a little bowl of salt water before the main course is served. You can serve them whole or slice them before dunking them in the salt water.

A Seder plate, or ka'arah—a large, round ornamental plate with six small sections. Each section holds a symbolic bit of food that helps tell the story of Passover.

Stocking the Seder Plate

A roasted egg. This particular egg is purely symbolic and is not eaten. A helpful hint: Do not roast a raw egg! Hard boil it before roasting it in a small pan with a bit of oil, unless you enjoy cleaning exploded albumen stuck to the inside of your oven. You can also get a little char on the shell by holding a hard-boiled egg over a gas stovetop flame with tongs until it starts to turn brown and crack.

A roasted lamb shank bone. The part of the lamb from the knee joint to just below it, this is also highly symbolic and not for eating. It should be carefully roasted to ensure that some of the meat remains on the bone, though traditions vary. Some supermarkets give these away for free before Passover. A roasted chicken neck or bone may also be used. Vegans and vegetarians can substitute a roasted carrot or beetroot.

Horseradish. Get a raw, knobby horseradish root with a green top to sit on the Seder plate. From the bottom, chop or slice enough pieces (they should be roughly the size of an olive) so that each guest has two. Some guests may clamor for more. If you plan on serving gefilte fish, you can also get grated horseradish in a jar, like Gold's—the red kind, with beets, or the white one without. Better still, get both!

Peter Himmelman

You won't find singer/songwriter/composer/author Peter Himmelman on tour during Passover. Nor does he accept gigs on any of the high holidays or Shabbat. During these times, he's home with family. Married to Bob Dylan's daughter Maria since 1988, this may include their four grown kids and two young grandkids.

Born and raised in a secular Jewish family, Himmelman didn't become observantly Jewish until well into adulthood. He pinpoints Pesach, however, as a locus of his spiritual consciousness long before that.

"I didn't know anyone who took religion seriously," he says of his childhood in St. Louis Park, Minnesota. "Any talk of God would've cast me as someone who had to go to one of Minneapolis's psychiatric hospitals." Yet that's exactly what a teenage Himmelman did during a Seder. When a scientist family member gave a scientific critique of the plague of frogs, Himmelman clapped back, irate that no one at the table was capable of suspending disbelief. "The wonderment of 'How does all this stuff [on Earth] get here? Where do you go when you die?' Nothing I'd ever heard explained it well," he says. "It's not answerable. That's the beauty of it."

At age twenty-three, shortly after his father died, Himmelman found himself back in St. Louis Park, walking down the street on a Passover eve and observing that his not-very-observant Jewish neighbors had all been celebrating. "I remember seeing a friend's mom vacuuming after their Seder and thinking, 'How is it that these people—three thousand three hundred years after the event—are still having a Seder and eating matzah?'" he says. "[I thought,] 'What is with these people that I belong to? What is the strength?' It's about memory. Jews are people of long memory." That realization, he says, "gave me goose bumps at the time, and it still does."

Himmelman did a scholarly exploration of his own religion, which turned into practice, from holiday rituals to observing the Sabbath each week. "We're among the only people in the world who ritualistically shut off their phones," he says. "I can't say that it's better, but it is differentiating."

Connecting his rock 'n' roll life and his spiritual life, though, is not a stretch for Himmelman, from the mysteries of songwriting and music itself ("Really great musicians transcend the merely rational," he says) to the dissident overlap of rock and Judaism. "Rock 'n' roll's intent was subversive," he says. "Judaism was trying to subvert something, too—whether it was in Rome, or Greece, or today, in any of the big societies—the idea that there was something that transcended human accomplishment."

Charoset. This mixture of chopped apples, nuts, spices, and wine is explained below. Put a little bit of it in a small dish for the Seder plate and the rest in a larger bowl to pass around, enough for everyone to have a couple of spoonfuls.

Romaine lettuce. Separate, wash, and dry enough leaves for every guest to have at least one.

Parsley. Wash and dry a bunch of fresh sprigs, enough for each guest to have at least one large sprig.

A main dish for the shulchan orech. Traditionally, this is brisket and/or chicken (and lamb for Sephardim), with vegetable sides such as tzimmes (root vegetables stewed with dried fruit), kugel (a starch-and-egg-based casserole), and matzah ball soup and gefilte fish to start. Of course, you can make it veggie or vegan or anything you prefer.

Consider stockpiling seltzer for the prolonged, salty evening ahead!

If you can, provide each guest with an extra pillow or cushion to embrace the custom of "reclining" at the Seder. In ancient times, lying on one's side while eating and drinking signified freedom. Some Seders are conducted while reclining on the floor, and there's no shame in that game. The **"Gangsta Lean"** ♪—always to the left (it's traditional and medicinal)—during the course of the evening is encouraged and, at points, commanded. At the very least, the host of the Seder should have a **"Lean on Me"** ♪ pillow on their chair as a symbol of this notion.

Getting Rid of Chametz:
Goodbye to You

Chametz is any grain—wheat, rye, barley, etc.—that has had contact with water for eighteen minutes or more, which is when leavening begins. Yeasts and sourdough starters are chametz, too, and so are fermented drinks made with grain; no **"Beer Drinkers & Hell Raisers"** ♪ are invited to this holiday (sorry, ZZ Top).

To avoid a Passover Scandal, religious Jews tell chametz **"Goodbye to You"** ♪ for the entire weeklong holiday. The most observant folks replace everything in their kitchen that has touched chametz, just for Pesach. Dishes, flatware, glasses, utensils, pots and pans, even small appliances are packed away, while larger appliances are lined or sealed off. **"It's Not Unusual"** 🎵 for observant Jewish families to have an entire kitchen's worth of stuff solely for use during Passover. Don't feel you have to keep up with the Tom Joneses, however; some folks use disposable plates and utensils instead, and some don't engage in these rituals at all.

The night before the first Seder, the entire home is checked for errant chametz. (When Pesach falls on a Saturday, this is done two nights before—on a Thursday—to avoid doing this work on Shabbat [the Sabbath].)

Look for things like the pretzel that slipped in between couch cushions, cookie crumbs on the shelf, and the random Cracker that rolled down **"Low"** under your desk. Make sure coat pockets are snack-free, too. Steely Dan's Jewish jazz/rocker Donald Fagen, who sometimes went by the punny name Illinois Elohainu (a play on "Adonoi Eloheinu," the Hebrew phrase for "Lord, Our God"), sang it: **"Everything Must Go."**

Hide-and-Seek Chametz:
Fun for the Whole Family!

File this under "Passover traditions wrapped in layers of symbolism": after the big purge, we actually hide some chametz around the house and invite the kids, or your favorite Stooges, to **"Search and Destroy"** 🎵 it.

You'll need stale bread, or any leavened goods you have on hand, wrapping that can safely be torched (like newspaper or a brown paper grocery bag), a long feather and a wooden spoon to ritualistically "sweep" out the chametz, matches, a single-wick candle, and a **"Flashlight"** 🎵 for kids (and for places in your home where you'd rather not take a burning candle).

Prepare ten **"Small Packages"** (giving Waylon Jennings vibes) of chametz, and make sure they're intact to contain the crumbs. The number ten is significant in Kabbalah lore, and they can be very small parcels (e.g., a crouton). The night before Passover, stash them around the house, turn off the lights, gather the family, and recite the bracha:

בָּרוּךְ אַתָּה יְיָ, אֱלֹהֵינוּ מֶלֶךְ הָעוֹלָם, אֲשֶׁר קִדְּשָׁנוּ בְּמִצְוֹתָיו, וְצִוָּנוּ עַל בְּעוּר חָמֵץ.

Baruch ata Adonoi, Elohaynoo Melech ha'olam, asher kidshanu b'mitzvotav v'tzeevanoo al bee'oor chametz.

Blessed are You, Adonoi our God, Ruler of the Universe, who sanctified our lives with commandments, and commanded us on the burning of chametz.

Now the search is on! Using the candle, flashlight, or both to light your way in the darkness, have everyone look for the ten packets, plus any other chametz you may have missed. When all have been gathered, recite this disclaimer, aka a "nullification incantation":

כָּל־חֲמִירָא וַחֲמִיעָא דְּאִכָּא בִרְשׁוּתִי דְּלָא חֲמִתֵּיה
וּדְלָא בְעַרְתֵּיה וְלֶהֱוֵי לִבְטֵל הֶפְקֵר כְּעַפְרָא
דְּאַרְעָא.

Kol chameera vachamee'a d'eeka virshutee d'la chameetay ud'la vi'artay livteel v'lehevay hefker k'afra d'ar'a.

Anything leavened that is in my possession, that I have not seen or not removed, shall be unclaimed and considered as the dust of the earth.

The morning of Passover, after you've eaten breakfast—the last chametz meal until after the holiday—place your ten packages, along with any breakfast refuse, outside in a safe firepit or grill and torch that toast!

Your home is now officially cleansed and ready for Pesach. You don't have to be one of the Kings of Leon to relish a little rock 'n' roll **"Pyro."**

There are many customs involved in this ritual. Some folks say the brachot before and after burning the chametz. Some add a prayer asking God for spiritual assistance while their chametz is ablaze. Some burn theirs at precisely five hours after sunrise on the 15th of Nisan. Some also "sell" their chametz before the holiday to cover anything they might miss. It's another symbolic gesture to show that you're all in, or, more specifically, all out. Technically, a non-Jew must "own" your chametz, so write up a bill of sale and hand it to a non-Jewish friend or neighbor in exchange for **"Money (Dollar Bill Y'all)"** that you'll return after the holiday. Rabbis will do this for you, too, and Chabad has an online form you can fill out to sell your chametz virtually and free of charge.

Like all Jewish rituals, this one has a deeper, intangible significance. Some rabbis speak of "spiritual chametz," which may refer to any unfortunate quality that distends our mind, ego, or spirit the way leavening puffs up bread—like conceit, envy, or arrogance. As you watch **"The Flame"** turn your bread into ash, reflect upon letting go of whatever "bloat" is bothering you. This is no Cheap Trick! Spring is a time of renewal, after all—even personal renewal. Getting rid of chametz can be very cathartic. Not only will your house be in a New Order, without **"Temptation,"** but your mind will be as well.

How the Haim Family Seder Inspired a Scene in the Film *Licorice Pizza*

The Shabbat dinner scene in Paul Thomas Anderson's *Licorice Pizza* is closely based on a Passover Seder that actually happened in the Haim family home. In her feature film debut, Alana Haim is surrounded by her real-life family—father, Moti (Mordechai); mom, Donna Rose; and sisters Danielle and Este, her cohorts in their band HAIM, all playing themselves.

In her Golden Globe–nominated performance, Haim plays Alana Kane, who brings a date to the Kanes' traditional Friday-night Shabbat meal. Moti asks if Alana's guest would like to say the blessing over the bread. He declines, stating that while he is Jewish, his "personal path" has led him to atheism.

Haim explains that "my middle sister [Este] was dating this guy that she brought to Passover, which is a huge deal. You're meeting not only my family but my extended family. We're all at my house to celebrate, and there's a tradition where you go around and you read a paragraph of the Haggadah, and it got to him and he respectfully refused, because he was an atheist. I think it was the most awkward Passover dinner I'd ever been to. I remember telling Paul that story, and then reading the script and being like, 'Huh; well, it's in the script.'"

Anderson captures every cringey feeling in the film. Alana yells at her dad, who calls her would-be beau an "idiot" for embarrassing her, and the sisters had a hard time keeping a straight face while shooting the scene. "I've never screamed at my dad ever," Alana says. "I think he was just shocked. But it was so funny."

Moti Haim was instrumental in his three daughters' music career. A pro soccer player and drummer who grew up in Jaffa, Israel, he formed their first family band in the mid-1990s called Rockinhaim. Donna Haim was in it, too. A Los Angeles transplant from Pennsylvania, her professional experience included winning *The Gong Show*. She played her Guild steel-string guitar and sang a Bonnie Raitt song, **"Blender Blues,"** with cheeky lyrics about whipping, chopping, and pureeing.

Donna also taught art to elementary school kids, including Paul Thomas Anderson, who discovered the connection only after hearing HAIM on the radio and meeting them. "I was in love with [Donna] as a young boy, absolutely smitten," he says. "She would sing songs during class, and she was the exact opposite of every other teacher. So that cemented the relationship in a pretty serious way.

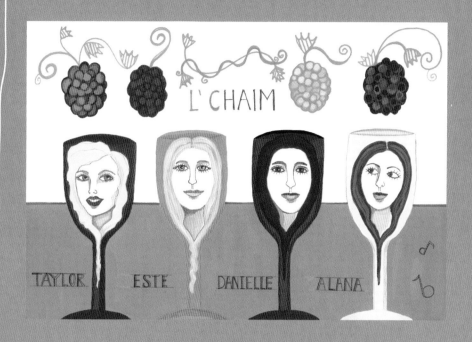

L'CHAIM

TAYLOR   ESTE   DANIELLE   ALANA

Our collaboration was more than just directing their music videos—our families became intertwined." (Anderson isn't Jewish, but his longtime partner, Maya Rudolph, is.)

As a band, HAIM's sunny, retro pop-rock (think Fleetwood Mac with hues of Ofra Haza and *NSYNC) caught the attention of another artist who soon became intertwined with their family—Taylor Swift. The sisters and the pop megastar quickly grew close after meeting in 2014. "It was just laughs, and I was like, 'Oh my God, you are literally one of us,'" Alana says. There were musical collaborations, parties, vacations, meeting each other's parents . . . and touring. HAIM joined Swift on the road for the latter's epic 2023 Eras Tour and performed some of their songs together. The trio even reprised their roles as Swift's evil stepsisters in the music video for **"Bejeweled"** (from 2022's *Midnights*), a *Cinderella* retelling written and directed by Swift.

Taylor Swift's "No Body, No Crime," featuring HAIM, is a murder mystery with Este Haim written into the lead role; it begins with the friends meeting up for wine.

How to Host a Seder

A Haggadah is the key to hosting a Seder. It's essentially a guide to the evening. The word "Haggadah" means "telling" in Hebrew, as you'll be telling a story, but it also contains the brachot, as well as detailed instructions on what to say, eat, and drink, and when to do these things. The word "Seder" itself means "order," and the Seder commences with a recitation of the order of the night.

As the host, you function as a sort of emcee. Everyone at the table will have a Haggadah and follow along, but you lead the night and say the blessings. You may outsource these duties. As for telling the story of Passover, it's traditional to go around the table and have each guest read a passage or two. Encourage your guests to speak up if they have questions or think of something to add. Some of the most interesting Seder discussions come from this, and it's very much in keeping with Judaism's culture of scholarly analysis of things large and small.

It's also customary to invite guests to your Seder who have nowhere else to go, or who have never attended a Seder, or to invite non-Jews who want to experience one of our most renowned holidays to join you and your family and friends. Take some extra time to explain the various rituals and traditions and how they relate to the story of the exodus as the evening unfolds. This may happen extemporaneously, or as the host you may want to have a few anecdotes at the ready (this Haggadah has lots of them, too).

Part of feeling as if we had personally experienced the exodus is the lengthy wait between the beginning of the Seder and when the festive meal is served, leaving everybody with a **"Hungry Heart."** ♪ This time will be consumed by the storytelling, discussion, singing, and many brachot. For some, it's customary not to eat beforehand. Others may put out a little nosh and slosh as guests arrive to keep everyone in good humor.

How Rock 'n' Roll Is Your Seder?

With its long trajectory of bizarre appetizers followed by a lavish repast, drenched in copious cups of wine, consumed on a pillowy incline while singing erupts throughout, a Seder falls somewhere between a *Beggars Banquet* and a bacchanalian feast. Like a musical performance, it may be very structured, with everyone following the same score, or more freewheeling, where participants are encouraged to jam. It can be as theatrical as a Queen song, involving all the senses. We don't just talk about tears and bitterness and sweetness—we see them, hold them, and taste them.

As a host, you set the mood, starting with your table. Beyond the Seder plate, it can be fine china on white tablecloths or skull-and-crossbones dinnerware on a royal purple runner, crystal goblets or an AC/DC chalice. Crystal goblets and silver candlesticks lend a certain Mick Jagger/Stevie Nicks vibe, but do what works for you: vintage or modern, or a mix.

Some families dress formally for a Seder, and some keep it casual. Observant hosts may wear a kittel, a white linen or cotton robe that's also utilized on high holy days and as a burial shroud, adding a bit of mysticism to the evening. Other traditional Jewish garb includes the yarmulke, or kippah, a skullcap worn by Orthodox men in deference to God looking down upon all our heads (Orthodox married women cover their heads as well). Kippot range from simple satin, velvet, or leather beanies often handed out to guests at Jewish weddings and bar/bat mitzvahs to the colorfully embroidered flat-top Bukharan-style yarmulke to crocheted, dome-hugging lids sporting the name of your favorite rock band and beyond. Rapper Kosha Dillz dons a Moses costume to host his Seders (more on this later). Wear whatever helps create the atmosphere you want.

For crafters, or those who'd like to do some fun Passover-related projects with kids, try making your own rock 'n' roll Seder plate out of a vinyl record. Place six small bowls in a circle on one side of a record that you're not likely to want to play again; matzah crumbs and sacramental wine are not easy to get out of the grooves. Or build a matzah pyramid centerpiece (by the way, the Giza pyramids predate the sojourn of the **"Israelites"** 𝄞 in Egypt by about a millennium; it's widely agreed upon that Jews did not build them). Notoriously crumbly, unleavened bread can make for a difficult medium, so if you can't shape it to your will, use mini-matzahs or nonedible crafting material. Be creative! Decorate it for your rock 'n' roll Seder with toy guitars, plectrums (guitar picks), a desert scene, or whatever else rocks your table.

How's your singing voice? You don't have to be mellifluous like a cantor to sing Passover songs. Sing like your favorite singer. Sing like Bob Dylan if you can, or Carole King, or Lou Reed, or Madonna, or Harry Styles. If you're new to this and never learned the classic melodies for the songs, look on YouTube to learn a few. You'll find everything from rabbis reciting brachot to celebrities such as Mayim Bialik singing "Chad Gadya" in Yiddish to Seders in their entirety. You'll also find plenty of song parodies, like **"Pesach Funk"** (Bruno Mars and Mark Ronson's **"Uptown Funk"**), **"Now We've Got Matzo"** (Taylor Swift's **"Bad Blood"**), **"Passover Rhapsody: A Jewish Rock Opera"** (Queen's **"Bohemian Rhapsody"**), the Shlomones' **"I'm Going to a Seder"** (the Ramones' **"I Wanna Be Sedated"**)—these might inspire you to come up with your own.

Honorable Menschen

Matzo and Metal—the Most Rock 'n' Roll Seder Ever

It happened one Pesach.

In 2005, VH1 gathered some of heavy metal's Jewish VIPs for a television special, *Matzo and Metal: A Very Classic Passover*. Scott Ian (Scott Ian Rosenfeld) of Anthrax, Jay Jay French (John French Segall) and Dee Snider (Daniel Snider, whose dad was Jewish) of Twisted Sister, and Leslie West (Leslie Abel Weinstein) of Mountain, sat down for a kosher dinner and discussion in Las Vegas. Ian, whose band rocked a **"Hava Nagila"** riff on their 1987 rap-metal song **"I'm the Man,"** went *Back to the Desert* (as in the Vegas Mandalay Bay Resort) for a sequel the following year. He was joined by Evan Seinfeld of Biohazard, Josh Silver of Type O Negative, and VH1 Classic host Lynn Hoffman. The episodes confirmed that at the heart of both Passover and rock 'n' roll is great storytelling.

Traditional foods:
History, Geography

Though we're all from the same tribe, most of modern Jewry is divided into two ethnic identities: the Ashkenazim, who landed in medieval western Germany and central and eastern Europe, and the Sephardim, whose roots are Iberian and Middle Eastern. (There are also Mizrahi Jews, Beta Israel Jews, and Romaniote Jews, among other subsets.) These distinctions were shaped by thousands of years of persecution and immigration, influencing the way Jewish holidays were conducted, even today.

The practices of each group differ, particularly when it comes to dietary matters, and both Ashkenazic and Sephardic Jews have representative cuisines. The brisket, gefilte fish, kugels, and tzimmes we eat on many holidays are generally (not exclusively) Ashkenazi. They're based on the foods that were commonly available in Europe as well as local culinary customs, and the way Jews incorporated them into a kosher diet. Cold climes yielded hearty fare, rich in meat cooked with fruit and root vegetables, dairy (not with meat, of course!), eggs, and dried, pickled, and smoked things that required preserving to consume during long winters.

Sephardim enjoyed warmer year-round weather and relatively healthier, spicier cuisine, based on kitniyot (grains, beans, legumes, and seeds), raw and cooked vegetables, olive oil, and savories like scallions and garlic. They don't remove kitniyot from their Passover table; it's too essential a part of their food intake, so it became traditional to include them during the weeklong holiday.

Jews would historically let local spiritual leaders figure out halacha and then explain how it translated to real life. Medieval rabbis in Europe, for example, thought kitniyot looked too much like chametz and would confuse those who were readying for Pesach, so they banned it from the holiday, a practice that continues among some descendants of Ashkenazim. And unlike Ashkenazim, Sephardim include lamb on their Seder menu—as long as it's not roasted.

But Ashkenazic and Sephardic Jews are no longer as separated as they once were. They live in the same cities and countries, their families are blended, and they have greater access to one another's practices than ever. A growing interest in Levantine, vegan, and gluten-free food has made Seder fare increasingly diverse. Based on all of this, the Rabbinical Assembly of Conservative rabbis deemed kitniyot kosher for Pesach in 2015 for those Ashkenazim who want it. These holidays don't have to be an all-or-nothing situation. Anything you do to celebrate is better than not doing anything at all.

Kosher for Passover

Come springtime, you'll see certain foods and beverages marked with "kosher for Passover" or "OKP" alongside the usual kosher endorsements. This means these consumables have been made and packaged in a place that follows the rules of kashruth, and may be eaten by observant Jews, and anyone else, of course. If you're invited to a Seder, check to see if the host keeps kosher and make sure anything you bring has the right endorsements—there are a number of organizations that award different symbols to manufacturers. Ask your host which ones are acceptable—one person's kosher may be another one's trayf (a way of saying "not so kosher").

Certain products are available only around the holiday. You might see them here and there during the year, but they're most readily available around Passover, including coconut macaroons, matzah, and kosher for Passover Coke, with its seasonal yellow cap. Like Mexican Coke, it's made with cane sugar instead of corn syrup, and is a favorite among soda devotees and home cooks alike (it's also great for braising brisket). To paraphrase Snoop Dogg, ain't nothin' but a P thing, baby.

Joyva:
A Ukrainian Immigrant, a Generational Business, a Passover Tradition

After immigrating to New York City from a small town just outside of Kyiv in 1907, Nathan Radutzky started out selling halvah—a Middle Eastern confection with a fudge-like texture made of sweetened crushed sesame seeds, sometimes swirled or coated with chocolate or dotted with almonds. The recipe traveled with the twenty-one-year-old from Ukraine to the Lower East Side. From a pushcart and a small storefront on Orchard Street, a multigenerational family business was born. By 1931, Radutzky had a factory built in Bushwick, Brooklyn, where it remains today. He also had four kids with his wife, Ray. The Joyva brand (introduced in 1951) was named after his granddaughter Roslyn Joy combined with a bit of the word "halvah."

The demand for confections had always been big, but Radutzky found another niche—Passover candies. Radutzky started making Jelly Bars during the 1930s to meet the clamoring for Passover sweets. By the 1960s, Joyva bought a starch mogul machine—new technology that allowed them to cut the jelly bars into shapes—and the iconic jelly ring was born. Jell Rings are enrobed in bittersweet chocolate, alongside their candy cousin, Joyva's Marshmallow Twists. Though now available

Gefilte fish vs. the Band Phish

Gefilte fish is as polemic as the band Phish: most people really like it or really don't.

Gefuelten hechden, or stuffed pike, was a popular Lenten dish among Catholics in medieval Europe before it migrated into Jewish gastronomy. Its mid-twentieth-century iteration was akin to spongy fish globs suspended in jars of goo (actually just jelled broth). Yet its Jewish history is complex and consequential, a food born of poverty (it could be made with fish heads and bones) that satisfied religious requirements (no cooking on holy days) and held mystical symbolism (fertility, good omens). Bubbes (grandmas) migrated to the United States clutching their shissels, big bowls used to separate fish bones from flesh (again, not on holy days!), and stocked their tenement bathtubs with live carp waiting to be "gefilted."

Both gefilte fish and Phish have large Jewish fan bases. The fish appears as a first course on some Jewish holidays, including Shabbat. The band has appeared on some Jewish holidays, working songs such as **"Yerushalayim Shel Zahav"** and prayers like Avinu Malkeinu into their set; they've even performed "Dayenu" and "Chad Gadya" when their shows coincided with Passover. And unlike the fish, Phish has Jewish roots—both bassist Mike Gordon and drummer Jon Fishman are members of the tribe.

Was Elvis Jewish?

Ever wonder why Elvis wore a chai and a Star of David in his later years? He'd wear a cross, too. "I don't want to get left out of heaven on a technicality," he joked. The King had tremendous spiritual curiosity, but he also had Jewish roots—his maternal great-great-grandmother, Nancy Burdine, was Jewish. He had a Star of David carved on his mother Gladys Presley's gravestone, as she was said to be proud of their heritage. He was also known to support

Jewish charities and causes. His chai, custom designed with seventeen diamonds, remains on display at Graceland.

Elvis's affection for Judaism, though, goes beyond his DNA—and his flashy jewelry. In the early 1950s, the Presleys rented an apartment in a two-family house at 462 Alabama Avenue in Memphis. Their upstairs neighbors were a young Orthodox rabbi, Alfred Fruchter, his wife, Jeanette, and their kids. The families became friendly, with the Fruchters often hosting Elvis and Gladys for meals and Jewish holidays.

Jeanette was very fond of Elvis. "He was one of the biggest mensches I've ever known," she said. "He was so respectful, too." He called Alfred "Sir Rabbi."

After observing the Jewish family for a while, the teenager began to do things around the house for them on Shabbat—things observant Jews are prohibited from doing (such as turning on lights). Technically, Jews can't ask someone to do these things, though they may drop hints. Elvis understood, but when the Fruchters offered him money for helping out, he refused.

The rabbi and his family found other ways to pay back Elvis's kindness. They'd sometimes take care of the Presleys' water bill. They let Elvis borrow their record player for as long as he wanted (he didn't own one at the time). And when he graduated from high school, Jeanette bought him the onyx cuff links and tiepin he'd had his eye on as a graduation gift. She attended the ceremony, too.

Jeanette and Gladys often had coffee together and talked, the latter expressing concern about her son's future. "She wanted him to give up his singing career to become a doctor," Jeanette said. "But I told her she shouldn't worry. One day he would make her proud, no matter what career he chose."

Elvis did, of course. In the late 1950s, when the Fruchters had relocated to California, Alfred went to see Elvis perform and visited with him backstage. The now-famous singer greeted him warmly and introduced him around as "my rabbi."

Check with your rabbi before you make Elvis's famous peanut butter and banana sandwich on matzah during Passover! Some folks consider peanuts kosher for the holiday, and some don't.

year-round, generations of Jewish families made it a tradition to add these sweet treats with a history all their own to their Seders.

The jelly rings are sold in boxes of eighteen, or "chai" in Hebrew, an important number in Jewish lore as the word also means "life." (In the Hebrew alphabet, each letter has a numerical value: Chet ח is eight. Yud י is ten. Eight plus ten equals חי chai!) Jews often give gifts in multiples of eighteen dollars or wear a chai around their necks as a religious symbol. Did Radutzky or his sons, who lived long, fortunate lives, choose the number on purpose? "Not every secret has been passed from generation to generation," Richard Radutzky, third-generation owner and copresident, says. "It's possible that our ancestors put eighteen Jell Rings in a box because of chai, but we can't know for sure. Let's just call it a meaningful coincidence."

Matzah: Unleavened but Not Unloved

Mentored by a Jewish family—the Karnofskys—during his rough childhood in New Orleans, legendary jazz trumpeter Louis Armstrong picked up a few things: 1. a tin horn, soon to be swapped for a trumpet; 2. the song **"Russian Lullaby"** ♪ (after having dinner with the family, Armstrong would stay to hear Mrs. Karnofsky sing it while she tucked her baby David into bed); and 3. his love of snacking on matzah year-round.

Yes, matzah! The heavy-duty flatbread may be loaded with chopped liver or baba ghanoush, but it's also loaded with symbolism. When Pharaoh agreed to free the Jews in Egypt, they wanted to get out. There was no time for their bread to rise, so instead of **"Running on Empty"** ♪ they grabbed the unleavened loaves and tossed them on their backs as they left. Under the desert sun, the "bread" baked into the crisp matzah we eat on Passover to remember the persecution Jews suffered.

Some love the "bread of affliction," and for some, it causes actual affliction on the digestion or dental work. It may be found in regular wheat, whole wheat, egg, or gluten-free varieties. There's also shmura matzah, handmade into beautifully uneven rounds and sold in pizza-box-like packaging. The grain that goes into this super matzah is carefully monitored throughout every step of the manufacturing process to prevent any contact with water that would result in leavening; shmura means "guarded." It has a rustic, oven-singed taste and is worth seeking out. You can find it everywhere, from Jewish specialty bakeries to your local synagogues to Costco.

It's worth noting that all matzah was handmade until the mid-nineteenth century, when the first matzah-making machine was invented. That sparked more than a century of halachic debate on "man versus machine"—i.e., is it better, is it kosher, is it putting people out of work?

Jews are commanded to eat matzah only during the Seders, but there's plenty to do with extra. It can be made into post-Seder breakfasts of matzah brei (like unfluffy French toast), matzah "pizza" under layers of tomato sauce and mozzarella, dessert (e.g., covered in chocolate, toffee, and sea salt), broken into small bits (farfel) in a side dish of kugel, and pulverized (meal) to use the same way you'd use breadcrumbs. However you choose to use it, it's customary to avoid eating it before Passover to intensify the impact of that first bite at the Seder. For some, thirty days of pre-Pesach matzah abstinence is the tradition; your family or community may differ.

The Springsteen Seder

B ruce Springsteen is not Jewish, though his lyrics are steeped in theology, inspiring Rutgers professor of Jewish studies and author Azzan Yadin-Israel to write a book about Springsteen's biblical motifs that includes "The Springsteen Midrash." Among the Boss's vast catalog are many titles that relate to a rock 'n' roll Seder and Judaism: **"The Promised Land," "The River," "Spirit in the Night,"** and more, but they're really about the impact of his Catholic upbringing and, naturally, New Jersey.

While many fans describe his concerts as a "religious experience," one superfan, Warren Rosen, turned that metaphor into a reality in 2012 when he held a private Seder in a Madison Square Garden restaurant so as not to miss Springsteen's concert at the venue when Pesach fell on the same date. E Street Band saxophonist Jake Clemons stopped by and read from the customized Haggadah Rosen had created, which included the Boss's face on the cover, and the family sang their own parody of Springsteen's **"Wrecking Ball"** as "Matzo Ball."

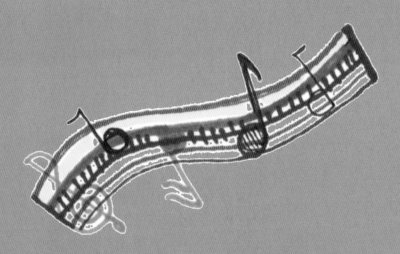

Max Weinberg: Give the Drummer Some

The only Jewish member of Bruce Springsteen's E Street Band, drummer Max Weinberg was bar mitzvahed in a black mohair suit—a decade before Elton John sang about one in "Bennie and the Jets." Weinberg attended Passover Seders in the lower level of the synagogue his family belonged to—the same room where he played many gigs as a teenager. "I think all music is connected to the [Jewish] concept that I grew up with, and that is tikkun olam—a pathway lighting [repairing] the world, making it better," he says. "When you are involved in a religious service, in a synagogue, in a church, in a cathedral, in a cave, or in a rock 'n' roll concert—a religious experience for some—at the best of times, you're transformed."

Max Weinberg uses the word "seder" to describe the order that a drummer keeps within a band.

Matzah Balls, Y'all

For such a simple food, the unassuming matzah ball has serious magnetism—enough to lure its fans to a dinner party where they will sit at a table and not eat for at least an hour. It has been a discipline in the wild world of competitive eating, with one of the all-time champions, Joey Chestnut, consuming seventy-eight of them in eight minutes. Thanks to jazz musician/polymath Slim Gaillard, **"Matzoh Balls"** even have a song they share with their pal, gefilte fish.

Like gefilte fish, matzah balls are thought to have been poached from European cuisine. The German knödel became the Yiddish kneidlach, made with ground matzah meal, egg, water, chicken fat (or a substitute), and salt and pepper. Versions may contain herbs and spices for flavor, and seltzer to make them float in a bath of luscious chicken soup. It's a big bowl of comfort that no Seder should be without.

Low Cut Connie's Kinky Pesach

Philadelphia-based musician Adam Weiner punctuates his sentences with Yiddish words like schlep, which means "to lug" or "drag" something cumbersome. Weiner would know; under his band name/alter ego Low Cut Connie, he has been schlepping a piano around the country, playing 1950s-inflected, barroom-bluesy, barrelhouse-boogie rock 'n' roll. Why haul his own piano? All the better to leap atop of in his boots during his high-octane performances, like rock icons Jerry Lee Lewis and Little Richard before him.

On tour for the last decade and a half or so, Weiner says the uptick in antisemitism has been palpable. His response, though, is to lean into his Jewishness—to be louder and prouder. He keeps finding more common ground between his religion and rock 'n' roll. In a 2023 video for his song **"King of the Jews,"** 𝄞 Weiner appears wrapping himself in tefillin, a ritual involving two black leather boxes containing parchment scrolls with hand-scribed verses from Exodus and Deuteronomy. The boxes are attached to long leather straps that observant Jews bind themselves with during weekday prayer—one on the arm and one on the head. Weiner explains:

I grew up in a Conservative Jewish household—Hebrew school twice a week, Jewish camp, tefillin, bar mitzvah. We used to do these epic four-plus-hour Seders every Passover, reading every single page of the book [Haggadah] in Hebrew and English. It was long and exhausting with lots of dramatic inflections to tell the story.

I've never much thought of it before, but I guess that's where I get my sense of drama. Everything I do with my music and performance has this dramatic edge to it. I think as Jews we are all obsessed with death, and even in joyful moments we dwell on death. We don't celebrate holidays . . . we "observe" them.

Passover is yet another "let us describe all the ways they tried to kill us" holiday. We list all the traumas and then we eat. There's ram's blood and shank bones, and to be honest it's very kinky. Definitely the most rock 'n' roll of the Jewish holidays.

I love being a Jew. It's an attitude. It's a misfit mentality. As we say in Philly, "They don't like us, we don't care!" Our people have lived through it all. We're tough. And funny. And, ultimately, very sweet.

Lou Reed and the Legendary Downtown Seder

I n the early 1990s, New York concert promoter Michael Dorf began hosting an annual Downtown Seder for his Lower Manhattan mishpucha; the Yiddish word for family, mishpucha can also denote a network of close friends. Dorf's included Jewish music luminaries Lou Reed, John Zorn, and Philip Glass, among others. There was no question who he'd task with portraying the Wise Child: Lou Reed, a rock 'n' roll icon and one of its most brilliant, subversive, and prickly practitioners.

Reed was the cofounder and primary songwriter for the Velvet Underground, an arty, experimental ensemble that utilized theater, literature, film, poetry, free jazz, and instrumental drone in the mid-1960s. Pushing the limits of what rock 'n' roll could (and would) be, the band's albums sold poorly, but its impact on future generations of musicians is incalculable. Reed found chart success in the 1970s with his solo work, only to follow it up with the audacious *Metal Machine Music*, a double album of electronic noise, along with a descent into drug use that began in his teen years. He returned to hitmaking in the 1980s and re-formed the Velvet Underground in the 1990s. In the aughts, Reed made a concept album based on the

work of Edgar Allan Poe, collaborated with Metallica (his last work before his death in 2014), and married avant-garde multimedia artist Laurie Anderson. Over a period of five decades, he often surprised and shocked as an artist. He also made some of rock's most influential albums, including *The Velvet Underground & Nico* and his second solo album, *Transformer*.

For this visionary boundary-pushing and artistic authority, Dorf asked Reed to cover the Haggadah section that represents the Seder's most enlightened participants. "What I did, and what we still do, was to allocate parts of the Haggadah to folks for them to interpret, to do anything

40

they felt represented their section," Dorf says. Rather than read from the traditional text, Reed would recite lyrics from his own work, such as "Teach the Gifted Children" (from his 1980 album *Growing Up in Public*), or Bob Marley's "Exodus," or Poe's "The Raven" (Reed also wrote poetry throughout his life).

Of the artists' contributions, Dorf says, "Some of it was communal, some was performance." Genre-defying saxophonist/composer John Zorn played the Wicked Child. Philip Glass, the vastly influential minimalist pianist/composer, played his "Etude No. 6." Hal Willner, celebrated producer of artists from Reed to Lucinda Williams, read Beat poet Allen Ginsberg. (The son of a Holocaust survivor, Willner was in charge of the sketch music on *Saturday Night Live* from 1980 until his death from COVID-19 in 2020.) Film clips intersected the evenings with spiritual leaders and activists such as Martin Luther King Jr. and artists in absentia. It was a multimedia experience, from the literary expressions to the food. "The first year, I assigned 'matzah' to a dancer, and she ended up putting matzah all over the stage and dancing on it," Dorf says. "There was matzah flying everywhere; it was crazy."

First held at Dorf's Tribeca club, the Knitting Factory, the Downtown Seder is an extension of what the concert promoter has always served club-going New Yorkers. "We're supposed to tell the story of the exodus from Mitzrayim in the language we understand," Dorf says. "For us, that's the language of the arts—music, humor, poetry, dance, short film—all of that." Now hosted at Dorf's City Winery venues in New York, Chicago, Atlanta, and other cities, the annual Passover celebration has grown to include comedians, politicians, and other celebrities. They've come to add what Dorf calls Four More Questions—"in other words, what are the bigger questions that we should be asking right now?" he says.

For Reed, who used to say that his only God was "rock 'n' roll," the Seder appealed on many levels. "Passover themes are incredibly transcendental," Dorf says. "The Seder appealed to his universal sense of being human, the themes of emancipation and freedom, both external and internal." The interpretive and experimental approach to the holiday resonated with Reed, who often brought family members to the Downtown Seders, as did the practice of an ancient ritual with a culinary manifestation. "Some say the Last Supper was a Seder. It's the world's most famous dinner party, and Lou loved dinner. After shows he loved to take his band to dinner," Dorf, who connected with Reed not only via music but over their shared love of wine, says.

"He was a deep, spiritual guy. He was not religious and didn't attend other holidays," Dorf says. "But he knew where he came from. He understood the relationship between the Jewish faith and the universal quality that is New York, that borrows from all these different worldly cultures. And Judaism is a part of it."

Anatomy of a Seder Plate

At the head of every Passover table, in front of whoever is conducting the Seder, is the Seder plate with its symbolic foods:

Shank bone (z'roah/זְרוֹעַ): The small roasted lamb shank symbolizes the sacrifice of the paschal lamb (korban pesach). The lamb's blood was painted on the doorways of Jewish homes so the Angel of Death would know to "pass over" them during the tenth plague of slaying of the firstborn, hence the name of this holiday. Some say the z'roah—which means arm—represents the "strong hand and an outstretched arm" of God that liberated us from Mitzrayim.

Roasted egg (beitza/בֵּיצָה): The egg is symbolic of many things: the festival sacrifice (korban chagigah), mourning, the cycle of life, hope for the future, and more.

Bitter herb (maror/מָרוֹר): The bitter herb symbolizes the bitterness of the lives and **"Bitter Tears"** 🎵 of Jews in Egypt. It is represented by raw horseradish root, which some Seder-goers like to consume INXS.

Green vegetable (karpas/כַּרְפַּס): The green vegetable (parsley or something similarly verdant) symbolizes springtime, as well as a connection to the story of Joseph and the fertile section of Egypt where the Israelites farmed for generations before the era of a cruel pharaoh.

Chazeret/חֲזֶרֶת: Aka more maror. This is a second bitter herb, usually played by romaine lettuce. It's used as a vehicle for the charoset as well.

Charoset/חֲרֹסֶת: A mix of chopped apples, nuts, and wine, charoset symbolizes the **"Bricks and Mortar"** 🎵 made by enslaved Jews in Egypt.

What's the Deal with Charoset?

It's the color of bricks and represents the construction mortar used by Jewish laborers in Egypt. The Ashkenazi version is coarsely chopped apples, walnuts, honey, red wine, and cinnamon, while Sephardim include raisins, figs, or other fruits and spices. The good thing is that it's hard to mess up. Brown sugar or agave, cardamom or thyme, apricots or pears . . . experiment with your own.

The Seder Begins

On the eve of Passover, when your guests have arrived:

First, Light the Candles

Benching licht ("candle lighting") is part of many Jewish holidays and has profound symbolic meaning. Generally done eighteen minutes before sundown, the light ushers in a divine presence and separates the rest of this day from what we're about to embark upon. We equate the candle's flame with joy and the ephemeral nature of being human. Candlesticks are often precious objects in Jewish families, handed down from generation to generation. They also worked pretty well before electricity, when the other option was to eat like Billy Squier: **"In the Dark."** 𝄞

Before everyone takes a seat, it's traditional to gather around the matriarch of the house—or the person of your choosing—for this ritual. The candles may be lit by one person, or more if desired. Other guests may participate in welcoming in the flame and then reciting the blessing together.

Lighting of the candles: With palms facing you and fingertips toward each other, move your hands from the candles toward your face in a circular motion, as if you're pulling the candle energy inward. Do this three times, then place your hands over your eyes (gently, if you need to read the prayer!) and say the following:

בָּרוּךְ אַתָּה יְיָ, אֱלֹהֵינוּ מֶלֶךְ הָעוֹלָם, אֲשֶׁר קִדְּשָׁנוּ בְּמִצְוֹתָיו וְצִוָּנוּ לְהַדְלִיק נֵר שֶׁל [שַׁבָּת וְשֶׁל] יוֹם טוֹב.

Baruch atah Adonoi, Elohaynoo Melech ha'olam, asher kid'shanoo b'mitzvotav v'tzeevanoo l'hadleek ner shel [Shabbat v'shel*] Yom Tov.

Blessed are You, Adonoi our God, Ruler of the Universe, who sanctified us with commandments and commands us to kindle the lights of [Shabbat and†] the Festival day.

Everyone takes a seat. Pour the first cup of wine, but don't drink it yet.

---

*   Add these words when Passover falls on a Friday night (erev Shabbat).
†   Add these words when Passover falls on a Friday night (erev Shabbat).

Pink Benches Licht

A crobatic pop singer Pink was on her 2013 tour, winding her way through the northeastern United States, when she realized it was Passover. Though not very religious—she calls herself an "Irish-German-Lithuanian Jew"—she didn't want to let the holiday go unheralded. She gathered her drummer, fellow Jewish musician Mark Schulman, and they took a moment to celebrate. "Pink and I did a private lighting of the candles in her dressing room," Schulman says. "Neither of us are particularly practicing, but we do respect the roots and honor the roots. It was heartwarming to go in and say the prayer. She said the prayer and I was like, 'I'm impressed, girl. You know the bracha.'"

The Grammy-winning star was born Alecia Beth Moore to a Jewish mother, Judy Kugel, and a Catholic father, Jim Moore, a Vietnam veteran. They divorced when Pink was ten, and the fallout can be heard in some of her songs, like **"Family Portrait."** The future singer quickly took up smoking, getting high, and generally acting out. Kugel, an ER nurse and full-time student, wasn't having it; by the time Pink turned fifteen, her mom had kicked her out of the house.

Whether she's home or on the road, Pink shares Jewish traditions with her mom and her kids ... and sometimes her bandmates.

After a near-death experience, Pink got it together and put herself on the path to success. Though her family relationships were intermittently volatile, she and her mom eventually developed a close bond. Sharing glimpses of her life on Instagram, Pink's "mom posts" include preparation for Jewish holidays and a handwritten recipe for "Judy Kugel's KUGEL."

There hadn't been much room for religious practice in their lives, but Judy managed to instill a Jewish identity in her daughter. When Pink became a mother to Willow and Jameson (her kids with her racer husband, Carey Hart), she felt it important to pass that along. While on tour in 2017, she took the kids to Berlin's Holocaust Memorial, not far from the Brandenburg Gate and the wall that once divided Germany. Taking in the rolling, 204,000-square-foot labyrinth of coffin-like concrete slabs officially titled "Memorial to the Murdered Jews of Europe," six-year-old Willow had an epiphany: "Wait—so Mom-Mom [Judy] is Jewish. My mom's Jewish. Then I'm Jewish," she said. "Well, then this could have been us."

The next week, during a London tour stop, Pink asked her daughter which city she liked best. "I think it was Berlin," Willow said. "Because there was a wall and people were separated, and there was a war and people were killed, and now everybody's together and there's no more wall and there's no more war, and that means everything that's bad can be good again."

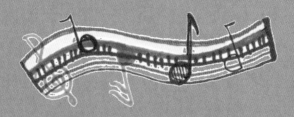

"Kadesh Urchatz," "קַדֵּשׁ וּרְחַץ" or "The Seder Song"

The order of the night is recited or sung together:

קַדֵּשׁ, וּרְחַץ, כַּרְפַּס, יַחַץ, מַגִּיד, רָחְצָה, מוֹצִיא מַצָּה, מָרוֹר, כּוֹרֵךְ, שֻׁלְחָן עוֹרֵךְ, צָפוּן, בָּרֵךְ ,הַלֵּל, נִרְצָה.

Kadesh, Urchatz, Karpas, Yachatz, Maggid, Rachtza, Motzi Matzah, Maror, Korech, Shulchan Orech, Tzafun, Barech, Hallel, Nirtzah.

The host then explains the meaning of each word.

קַדֵּשׁ— Kadesh (sanctify) is the kiddush, the blessing of the wine that begins holiday meals, including weekly Friday-night Shabbat dinners.

וּרְחַץ—Urchatz (and wash) is the first ritual washing of hands of the night, done prior to eating the green vegetable.

כַּרְפַּס—Karpas is a green vegetable, such as parsley.

יַחַץ— Yachatz (divide) is breaking the middle matzah in half.

מַגִּיד— Maggid is telling the story.

רָחְצָה—Rachtza is the second ritual washing of hands, this time before eating the matzah.

מוֹצִיא מַצָּה—Motzi Matzah is the Hamotzi, the blessing and eating of the matzah.

מָרוֹר— Maror is the blessing and eating of the bitter herbs.

כּוֹרֵךְ— Korech is the Hillel sandwich made with bitter herbs (we'll eat this later).

שֻׁלְחָן עוֹרֵךְ—Shulchan Orech is, at long last, the festive meal!

צָפוּן— Tzafun (hiding) precedes the eating of the afikomen (half of the matzah we divided earlier).

בָּרֵךְ— Barech is reciting the grace after meals (Birkat Hamazon).

הַלֵּל—Hallel is psalms of praise and songs (Psalms 113–18).

נִרְצָה—Nirtzah: the Seder concludes.

48

Kadesh: קַדֵּשׁ
Sanctifying the Festival with Wine

Adults (U don't need to B 40, just twenty-one in most states) are supposed to drink four full glasses of **"Red Red Wine"** 🎵 at the Seder, the significance of which is vast and varied. Scholars have come up with many interpretations of the four cups. Whether you line them up with four parts of the Seder, the Four Questions, the Four Children, the four matriarchs of the Jewish people, the four eras of mankind, the Fab Four (the Beatles), the Four Seasons (weather, or the band), the four weeks that the Bangles' **"Walk Like an Egyptian"** spent at number one on the *Billboard* Hot 100 chart, HAIM performing with Taylor Swift as a foursome, or just because you like wine, we start with the kiddush:

קַדֵּשׁ Sanctify

On Shabbat, begin here:

וַיְהִי עֶרֶב וַיְהִי בֹקֶר יוֹם הַשִּׁשִּׁי. וַיְכֻלּוּ הַשָּׁמַיִם
וְהָאָרֶץ וְכָל־צְבָאָם. וַיְכַל אֱלֹהִים בַּיּוֹם הַשְּׁבִיעִי
מְלַאכְתּוֹ אֲשֶׁר עָשָׂה וַיִּשְׁבֹּת בַּיּוֹם הַשְּׁבִיעִי מִכָּל
מְלַאכְתּוֹ אֲשֶׁר עָשָׂה. וַיְבָרֶךְ אֱלֹהִים אֶת יוֹם
הַשְּׁבִיעִי וַיְקַדֵּשׁ אוֹתוֹ כִּי בוֹ שָׁבַת מִכָּל־מְלַאכְתּוֹ
אֲשֶׁר בָּרָא אֱלֹהִים לַעֲשׂוֹת.

Va'ye'hee erev va'ye'hee voker yom ha-shee-shee.

Va'ye'chooloo hashamayeem v'haaretz v'chol tz'va'am. Va'y'chal Eloheem bayom ha'sh'vee'ee m'lach'to asher asah.

Va'yish'bot bayom ha'sh'vee'ee mee'kol m'lach'to asher asah. Va'ye'varech Eloheem et yom

ha'sh'vee'ee va'ye'kadaysh oto, kee vo shavat mee'kol m'lach'to asher bara Eloheem la'asot.

And there was evening and there was morning, the sixth day. And the heaven and the earth were finished, and all their host. And on the seventh day God finished His work which He had done; and God rested on the seventh day from all His work which He had done. And God blessed the seventh day, and sanctified it; because God rested on it from all of His work which God created in doing (Genesis 1:31–2:3).

On weekdays, begin here (Shabbat insertions are in parentheses):

סַבְרִי מָרָנָן וְרַבָּנָן וְרַבּוֹתַי. בָּרוּךְ אַתָּה יְיָ, אֱלֹהֵינוּ מֶלֶךְ הָעוֹלָם, בּוֹרֵא פְּרִי הַגָּפֶן.

Savree maranan v'rabanan v'rabotai.

With your permission, my teachers and rabbis.

Baruch ata Adonoi, Elohaynoo melech ha'olam, boray p'ree hagafen.

Blessed are You, Adonoi our God, Ruler of the Universe, who creates the fruit of the vine.

בָּרוּךְ אַתָּה יְיָ, אֱלֹהֵינוּ מֶלֶךְ הָעוֹלָם, אֲשֶׁר בָּחַר בָּנוּ מִכָּל־עָם וְרוֹמְמָנוּ מִכָּל־לָשׁוֹן וְקִדְּשָׁנוּ בְּמִצְוֹתָיו. וַתִּתֶּן לָנוּ יְיָ אֱלֹהֵינוּ בְּאַהֲבָה (לשבת: שַׁבָּתוֹת לִמְנוּחָה וּ) מוֹעֲדִים לְשִׂמְחָה, חַגִּים וּזְמַנִּים לְשָׂשׂוֹן, (לשבת: אֶת יוֹם הַשַּׁבָּת הַזֶּה וְ) אֶת יוֹם חַג הַמַּצּוֹת הַזֶּה זְמַן חֵרוּתֵנוּ, (לשבת: בְּאַהֲבָה) מִקְרָא קֹדֶשׁ זֵכֶר לִיצִיאַת מִצְרָיִם. כִּי בָנוּ בָחַרְתָּ וְאוֹתָנוּ קִדַּשְׁתָּ מִכָּל הָעַמִּים, (לשבת: וְשַׁבָּת) וּמוֹעֲדֵי קָדְשֶׁךָ (לשבת: בְּאַהֲבָה וּבְרָצוֹן) בְּשִׂמְחָה וּבְשָׂשׂוֹן הִנְחַלְתָּנוּ.

Baruch ata Adonoi, Elohaynoo melech ha'olam, asher bachar banoo mee'kol am, v'ro'me'manoo mee'kol lashon, v'kid'shanoo b'mitzvotav. Va'tee'ten lanoo, Adonoi Elohaynoo, b'ahavah mo'adim l'simchah, chagim ooz'manim l'sason, et yom chag Ha'matzot hazeh, z'man chay'roo'taynoo, mikra kodesh,

zay'cher lee'tzeet Mitz'ra'yim. Kee vanoo vacharta v'otanoo keedashta mee'kol ha'ameem umo'aday kod'shecha b'simchah oov'sason hinchaltanoo.

Blessed are You, Adonoi our God, Ruler of the Universe, who has chosen us from all peoples and has raised us above all language and has sanctified us with His commandments. And You have given us, Adonoi our God, [Sabbaths for rest], appointed times for happiness, holidays and special times for joy, [this Sabbath day, and] this Festival of Matzot, our season of freedom [in love] a holy convocation in memory of the Exodus from Egypt. For You have chosen us and sanctified us above all peoples. In Your gracious love, You granted us Your [holy Sabbath, and] special times for happiness and joy.

בָּרוּךְ אַתָּה יְיָ, מְקַדֵּשׁ (לשבת: הַשַּׁבָּת וְ) יִשְׂרָאֵל וְהַזְּמַנִּים.

Baruch ata Adonoi, m'kadaysh Yisrael v'ha'zma'neem.

Blessed are You, O Adonoi, who sanctifies [the Sabbath,] Israel, and the appointed times.

When Passover falls on a Saturday night, after Kiddush we add Havdalah, the blessing for the conclusion of Shabbat:

בָּרוּךְ אַתָּה יְיָ, אֱלֹהֵינוּ מֶלֶךְ הָעוֹלָם, בּוֹרֵא מְאוֹרֵי הָאֵשׁ. בָּרוּךְ אַתָּה יְיָ, אֱלֹהֵינוּ מֶלֶךְ הָעוֹלָם, הַמַּבְדִּיל בֵּין קֹדֶשׁ לְחֹל, בֵּין אוֹר לְחשֶׁךְ, בֵּין יִשְׂרָאֵל לָעַמִּים, בֵּין יוֹם הַשְּׁבִיעִי לְשֵׁשֶׁת יְמֵי הַמַּעֲשֶׂה. בֵּין קְדֻשַּׁת שַׁבָּת לִקְדֻשַּׁת יוֹם טוֹב הִבְדַּלְתָּ, וְאֶת־יוֹם הַשְּׁבִיעִי מִשֵּׁשֶׁת יְמֵי הַמַּעֲשֶׂה קִדַּשְׁתָּ. הִבְדַּלְתָּ וְקִדַּשְׁתָּ אֶת־עַמְּךָ יִשְׂרָאֵל בִּקְדֻשָּׁתֶךָ.

Baruch ata Adonoi, Elohaynoo melech ha'olam, boray m'oray ha'aysh.

Baruch ata Adonoi, Elohaynoo melech ha'olam, hamavdeel bayn kodesh l'chol, bayn or l'choshech, bayn Yisrael la'amim, bayn yom ha'sh'vee'ee l'shayshet y'may ha'ma'aseh. Bayn k'dooshat Shabbat lik'dooshat yom tov hivdalta. V'et yom ha'sh'vee'ee mee'sheishet y'may hama'aseh keedashta. Hivdalta v'keedashta et amcha Yisrael bik'doo'sha'techa.

Blessed are You, Adonoi our God, Ruler of the Universe, who creates the lights of the fire. Blessed are You, Adonoi our God, Ruler of the Universe, who distinguishes between the holy and the profane, between light and darkness, between Israel and the nations, between the seventh day and the six working days. You have distinguished between the holiness of the Sabbath and the holiness of the Festival, and You have sanctified the seventh day from the six working days. You have distinguished and sanctified Your people Israel with Your holiness.

בָּרוּךְ אַתָּה יְיָ, הַמַּבְדִּיל בֵּין קֹדֶשׁ לְקֹדֶשׁ.

Baruch ata Adonoi, hamavdeel bayn kodesh l'kodesh.

Blessed are You, Adonoi, who distinguishes between holy and holy.

No matter which kiddush we've just recited, we add the Shehecheyanu blessing here, the Jewish blessing for "firsts." We recite it whenever we engage in something for the first time that year, such as the first cup of wine on the first night of Passover, or the first fruit of a new harvest. No, you don't have to have harvested it yourself—even if you bought it at a market, a shehecheyanu is appropriate:

בָּרוּךְ אַתָּה יְיָ, אֱלֹהֵינוּ מֶלֶךְ הָעוֹלָם, שֶׁהֶחֱיָנוּ וְקִיְּמָנוּ וְהִגִּיעָנוּ לַזְּמַן הַזֶּה.

Baruch ata Adonoi, Elohaynoo melech ha'olam, she'heche'yanoo, v'kee'ye'manoo, ve'higee'anoo la'zman ha'zeh.

Blessed are You, Adonoi our God, Ruler of the Universe, who has kept us alive and sustained us and caused us to reach this season.

"Man, Oh Manischewitz!"

Manischewitz is the classic kosher wine that is both cherished and maligned. A Passover Seder without it has been unthinkable for nearly a century. This sacramental nectar is immortalized in popular culture, name-dropped in songs by artists from Incubus to NOFX to Sharon Jones. Manischewitz makes movie cameos, too: Joe Pesci's Tommy uses it to mock his Jewish date in *GoodFellas*, and Jack Black's Miles blames it for his boozy babbling in *The Holiday*. It has even been to the moon, when *Apollo 17* astronaut Eugene Cernan exclaimed "Manischewitz!" upon seeing something whiz by during his 1972 moonwalk; Cernan wasn't fond of cursing and often dropped the "M" word instead. It's so closely aligned with Judaism that it's practically a trope, yet most of its consumers—up to 80 percent—are not Jewish.

Sammy Davis Jr. embraced Judaism and kosher wine.

Manischewitz is more than just a wine. It's a culinary and cultural benchmark. The grape varietal for Jewish sacraments is Concord, the same grapes used to flavor jellies, pies, candies, juices, and other sweets. For many of us, these Concord-flavored products define what grapes taste like when we're young. So regardless of how sophisticated your palate may become, this humble kosher wine still gives the big, juicy grape flavor of childhood. It's made sweeter with the addition of corn syrup, which contributes to its consistency. For Passover, however, the company only uses pure cane sugar, as corn is kitniyot. We like to stock up on the sugar variety when we can.

But Manischewitz is so much more than that. It encompasses the American dream and the immigrant experience, the country's entrepreneurial spirit, its outlaw mythos, and its struggle between constitutionality and religious freedom. Yes, all of this is contained in a bottle of fermented grape juice.

As early as the turn of the twentieth century, the pipeline of Concord grapes flowed from upstate New York to Brooklyn, where they were fermented with rabbinical oversight to serve the growing influx of Jewish immigrants in need of kosher products. When the Constitution was amended to include Prohibition in

1919, language was written into the Volstead Act giving dispensation for sacramental wines, in limited amounts. Law enforcement pondered aloud how suddenly everyone was getting religious. Bootlegging rabbis were busted by Jewish G-men. Prohibition-touting politicians also played up anti-immigrant and antisemitic sentiments, labeling the liquor business a "foreign enterprise."

When Prohibition was repealed in 1933, Meyer Robinson of the Monarch Wine Company saw an opportunity. He leased the Manischewitz name from the family who owned the Manischewitz Company, a trusted producer of matzah and other kosher foods since 1888. Under the new moniker, Monarch grew to become one of the top five wine producers in the United States, including other wines like blackberry and elderberry, and sparkling and cream whites. Its Brooklyn winery occupied a massive four-city-block complex (where Industry City stands today). Later, its storage tanks gained a rock 'n' roll pedigree, as two of them were said to have originally been water tanks from the Woodstock festival.

Post–World War II, Robinson began to notice he was selling more product during Christmas and Thanksgiving than he did on Passover. Research revealed that the wine was popular among Black Americans. In the decades that followed, it became popular in growing Caribbean communities and was carried in Asian markets as well, being especially popular with Chinese American and Vietnamese American customers. With its sweet, juicy flavor profile and relatively low price point, Manischewitz became a wine of immigrants.

The company went all-in on marketing, making memorable ads with jazz great Billy Eckstine, as well as proto-doo-woppers the Ink Spots. ("Manischewitz Kosher Wine Harmonizes with Us—Sweetly! It's our favorite wine, too.") Radio announcers, including a pre–*Hogan's Heroes* Bob Crane, vocalized what became a classic tagline ingrained in pop culture: "Man, Oh Manischewitz!" In 1954, a Harlem doo-wop group called the Crows, backed by a group of players going under the name Melino and His Orchestra, released the Afro-Cuban-flavored **"Mambo Shevitz (Man O Man)"** 𝄞—part of a slim but entertaining volume of Jewish-Latin crossover music.

The ultimate brand ambassador, however, was entertainer Sammy Davis Jr.— Black, Jewish, and a paragon of cool. "Try some after dinner tonight," he says in an ad for the company's Cream Almonetta. "It's delicious!" A member of the Rat Pack, the actor/singer/dancer/comedian was multitalented with a nimble wit and always nattily dressed. He was friends with Sinatra and Elvis, with JFK and Nixon. A third-generation American born in Harlem in 1925, Davis hid his Cuban roots because of anti-Castro sentiment in the United States (claiming Puerto Rican heritage instead), but he fought racism throughout his life, making jokes in the face of incomprehensible stings. He began studying Judaism after losing his eye in a car accident and eventually converted, saying he identified with Jewish resilience.

53

GO AHEAD AND "CHUG-A-LUG" 🎼
THAT FIRST CUP LIKE "KING OF THE ROAD"
ROGER MILLER, AND DON'T FORGET
TO RECLINE WHENEVER YOU DRINK
WINE TONIGHT!

Urchatz: וּרְחַץ
The First Ritual Handwashing

Of course you should wash your hands before eating (because, ew), but ritual handwashing in Jewish ceremonies is symbolic. It requires a natla netilat yadayim, a specially sized, double-handled cup filled with water that you pour over alternating hands three times. Why the double handle? So as not to cross-contaminate your hands. Since we're big fans of the handwashing, we have an addiction to this *Ritual de lo Habitual*.

Some Seder hosts pass a big bowl around the table for guests to pour a little water on each hand, a custom descending from when folks had no indoor plumbing. It might be easier for everyone to get up and go to a sink to do this. No bracha is said during this first handwashing of the Seder.

Karpas: כַּרְפַּס
Dipping the Green Vegetable in Salt Water

Karpas represents springtime, in which Passover always occurs. Leaves return to trees, and greens are at their youngest and most tender. It's a time of eternal renewal and rebirth. It's also symbolic of the way Jews thrived in Egypt prior to being persecuted by this particular pharaoh, a family tree that grew countless branches, and the fertile soil of the Nile Delta that sustained us over centuries.

We dip the parsley in salt water, allegorical tears shed due to the hardships of Jewish life under a tyrannical, oppressive ruler. There were plenty of tears to go around in Mitzrayim at the time, and we dip for the suffering of all.

Dip the parsley in salt water, say this bracha, and then taste those tears. This may be read all together, or the host may read it:

בָּרוּךְ אַתָּה יְיָ, אֱלֹהֵינוּ מֶלֶךְ הָעוֹלָם, בּוֹרֵא פְּרִי הָאֲדָמָה.

Baruch ata, Adonoi, Elo'haynoo Melech ha'olam, boray p'ree ha'adamah.

Blessed are you, Adonoi our God, Ruler of the Universe, who creates the fruit of the earth.

Rashida Jones Finds the Afikomen

Rashida[*] Jones has starred in modern TV cult classics like *Parks and Recreation* and *The Office*, and in films such as *The Social Network*. She has written and produced films, winning a Grammy for Best Music Film for *Quincy*, a documentary about her legendary music producer/artist dad, Quincy Jones. She has a son, Isaiah, with longtime partner Ezra Koenig, singer of Vampire Weekend. (For his band's **"This Life"** video, Koenig filmed a star-studded rock 'n' roll Seder at Coachella, with Grammy-winning producer Mark Ronson—Jones's friend and former fiancé—at the head of the table.)

Ask her about her greatest moment, though, and she just might mention Passover.

"One year, when I was eight, I found the afikomen, and I got a bag of See's lollipops," she says. "That was probably the pinnacle of my life."

No doubt her *Angie Tribeca* character's dry humor is at play here, but Jones didn't grow up attending just any ordinary Seder. Her dad used to take the family to Chasen's for Passover. Located in West Hollywood, on the border of Beverly Hills, the eminent restaurant had a history of catering to the show biz elite. Its Seder was an annual ritual for some of the music industry's biggest executives and artists, including Quincy Jones. Her mom, actress/singer Peggy Lipton (*The Mod Squad, Twin Peaks*), was an Ashkenazi Jew, which Jones explored on the show *Who Do You Think You Are?*

Raised in a Los Angeles enclave that included other biracial and bireligious families (her friend, comedian/actor Maya Rudolph, daughter of producer Richard Rudolph and singer Minnie Riperton, lived nearby, along with actor Sidney Poitier and Joanna Shimkus, and filmmaker Sidney Lumet and Gail Jones), Jones was raised to embrace her cultural diversity.

"I just think about how ridiculous it is that I exist because the lineage on both sides, the probability that I would exist—a Black Jew in 2021—and succeed and thrive—is a miracle," Jones says. "And it's something I do not take for granted. I think about it constantly, every day. I don't understand why I was chosen, but I feel like I have to make good on my dad's survival and my family's survival."

---

[*] In Arabic, Rashida means "rightly guided." Rashid is a town in the Nile Delta. It's also known as Rosetta, where the Rosetta Stone—a key to unlocking Egyptian hieroglyphics—was discovered.

Yachatz: יַחַץ
Breaking the Middle Matzah

"Three Is a Magic Number," and not just for Blind Melon or in **"Schoolhouse Rock"** but in Judaism as well. Jews pray three times a day. There are three Jewish patriarchs: Abraham, Isaac, and Jacob. Moses was his parents' third child. The Torah was handed to him by God in the third month of the Jewish calendar. There are three pieces of matzah on the Passover table, in a stack, covered with a cloth.

Take the cover off the stack. Break the middle matzah roughly in half and place the smaller piece back between the other two. Wrap the larger piece in a napkin and put it aside—this is the afikomen.

(A note for the host: At some point, preferably when everyone at the table is distracted, hide the afikomen nearby for the kids, or whomever, to find later on. We'll eat it then.)

We save the bigger piece of matzah for after the festive meal to remind us that the best is yet to come, tonight, in life, and—if you're a believer—in the future when the messiah, aka Moshiach, arrives. (Jews are waiting for this to happen; our Supreme being just keeps us hangin' on.) We involve any kids present in the afikomen search and rescue to help keep them awake and engaged throughout this long night.

Yachatz symbolizes brokenness: Pharaoh's broken promises to the Israelites—first with enslavement, then vowing to let us go only to change his mind. The broken bodies of subjugation and toil. Broken hearts over babies drowned upon Pharaoh's order, and those firstborn sons taken by the Angel of Death during the tenth plague. Our own brokenness, both personal and from the tenets of Judaism.

Conversely, it also represents wholeness—the possibility of healing through the act of breaking bread together. We break up the smaller, or "poor," half of the middle matzah and pass it around the table. It commemorates the Israelites who shared their meager supplies with those less fortunate (and the many other times throughout history that Jews were rounded up and restricted). By the end of the festive meal, when we're no longer hungry and we're leaning on pillows like a boss, we'll break out the afikomen—the Big & Rich half of the middle matzah.

Maggid: מַגִּיד

Telling the Story of Passover

Ha Lachma Anya

Ha Lachma Anya is the only part of the Seder that's sung (or recited) not in Hebrew but in Aramaic—the common language of the era when the Jewish people were in Egypt. We're welcoming strangers to participate in our Seder using the historical vernacular so that they would've understood the invitation, or, to paraphrase Maude and the Dude in *The Big Lebowski*, in the parlance of their times. Most of us are not opening the door and yelling down the street. However, if you've already invited those with nowhere else to go, or if you've given tzedakah ("charitable donating with a moral imperative") to an organization that sponsors Seders for those who can't afford them, you've done a mitzvah and satisfied this portion of the reading. If not, there's always next year. Bonus: the last-minute invite is a real Passover thing. You can almost always find someone in need of a Seder to attend who lives in or is visiting your community.

Lift up the plate of matzah and say:

הָא לַחְמָא עַנְיָא דִּי אֲכָלוּ אַבְהָתָנָא בְּאַרְעָא דְמִצְרָיִם. כָּל דִּכְפִין יֵיתֵי וְיֵיכֻל, כָּל דִּצְרִיךְ יֵיתֵי וְיִפְסַח. הָשַׁתָּא הָכָא, לְשָׁנָה הַבָּאָה בְּאַרְעָא דְיִשְׂרָאֵל. הָשַׁתָּא עַבְדֵי, לְשָׁנָה הַבָּאָה בְּנֵי חוֹרִין.

Ha lachma anya dee'a'chah'loo av'hatana b'arah d'mitz'ra'yeem.

Kol dich'fin yay'say v'yay'chol, kol ditz'reech yay'say v'yif'sach.

Ha'shatah ha'cha, l'shah'nah ha'bah'ah b'ara d'yisra'el. Ha'shata avday, l'shah'nah haba'ah b'nay choreen.

This is the bread of affliction that our ancestors ate in the land of Egypt. Anyone who is hungry should come and eat; anyone who needs should come and partake of the Pesach sacrifice. Now we are here, next year we will be in the land of Israel; this year we are slaves, next year we will be free people.

POUR THE SECOND CUP OF WINE.

When Bob Dylan and Marlon Brando Crashed a Hollywood Seder

What would you do if the strangers who showed up at your Seder were a legendary rock 'n' roller and an iconic actor? It happened at Temple Israel of Hollywood in 1975. It seems Bob Dylan and Marlon Brando anonymously booked seats in advance and thrilled the rabbis and congregants when they arrived, accompanied by actress Helena Kallianiotes (who'd made her film debut in the Monkees' surrealistic, highly solarized *Head*), Dylan's first wife, Sara, and Dennis Banks, cofounder of AIM (the American Indian Movement).

Senior Rabbi Haskell Bernat introduced the celebrities, reminding everyone that welcoming "unexpected guests" is very much in the spirit of Passover, and reported afterward that the visitors participated throughout the evening. Brando recited the kiddush, and expressed his admiration for the Jewish people, the state of Israel, and the social activism of that particular synagogue.

Brando commented that he was delighted Rabbi Bernat was able "to use one of the world's most ancient religious ceremonies to highlight freedom movements today, including those of Soviet Jews, American Indians, and women." The activist actor drew parallels between "the awe and reverence for nature found in the American Indian religion and the humanitarianism of Reform Judaism." Dylan capped the night with a performance of **"Blowin' in the Wind"** as he launched the Birkat Hamazon (the grace after meals); the other Seder guests sang along, which is also very much in the spirit of the holiday.

When Harry Styles Is the Youngest Person at the Table

Hᵉ tweets in Yiddish and has a tattoo composed of Hebrew letters (it spells Gemma, his sister's name), but Harry Styles wasn't born Jewish. The spiritually minded pop star/actor immersed himself in Jewish culture after meeting Ben Winston. A producer and director, Winston helped usher Styles's former group, One Direction, to stardom. The band loved the "family vibe" that the Jewish Winston introduced them to. Styles even moved into the Winston family home for nearly two years, partaking in holidays including the Passover Seder. The youngest member of One Direction, Styles says that singing the Four Questions at the Seder table makes him nervous; youngest children everywhere who are called upon to sing in front of family and friends can relate to that.

Though Harry Styles says he is "more spiritual than religious," he has been known to tweet about Jewish holidays.

Why Is This Night Different from All Other Nights?

The Four Questions

There are actually five questions—the first one is rhetorical and the others are specific. Traditionally, the youngest person at the table asks them, but the idea is to engage all the children at the table (and all the adults as well) so they'll be interested in participating and learning. Some kids are shy and feel more comfortable with a little backup, so it's okay to ask or sing the questions as a group:

מַה נִּשְׁתַּנָּה הַלַּיְלָה הַזֶּה מִכָּל הַלֵּילוֹת?

Ma nishtanah ha'lai'lah hazeh mee'kol ha'laylot?

Why is this night different from all other nights?

שֶׁבְּכָל הַלֵּילוֹת אָנוּ אוֹכְלִין חָמֵץ וּמַצָּה, הַלַּיְלָה הַזֶּה – כֻּלּוֹ מַצָּה.

Sheb'khol ha'lay'lot anoo o'khleen chamaytz oo'matzah; ha'lai'lah hazeh, koolo matzah.

On all other nights we eat leavened products and matzah; on this night only matzah.

שֶׁבְּכָל הַלֵּילוֹת אָנוּ אוֹכְלִין שְׁאָר יְרָקוֹת – הַלַּיְלָה הַזֶּה (כֻּלּוֹ) מָרוֹר.

She'b'khol ha'lay'lot anoo okh'leen she'ar yerakot; ha'lai'lah hazeh, (koolo) maror.

On all other nights we eat all vegetables, and on this night only bitter herbs.

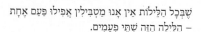

שֶׁבְּכָל הַלֵּילוֹת אֵין אָנוּ מַטְבִּילִין אֲפִילוּ פַּעַם אֶחָת
הַלַּיְלָה הַזֶּה שְׁתֵּי פְעָמִים. –

She'b'khol ha'lay'lot ayn anoo mat'beeleen a'filoo pa'am echat; ha'lai'lah ha'zeh, sh'tay f'amim.

On all other nights, we don't dip our food even once, and on this night we dip twice.

שֶׁבְּכָל הַלֵּילוֹת אָנוּ אוֹכְלִין בֵּין יוֹשְׁבִין וּבֵין מְסֻבִּין
הַלַּיְלָה הַזֶּה כֻּלָּנוּ מְסֻבִּין . –

She'b'khol ha'lay'lot anoo okh'leen bayn yosh'veen oo'vayn m'soo'been; ha'lai'lah hazeh, koolanoo mesoobeen.

On all other nights we eat sitting or reclining, and on this night we only recline.

The answers, though subject to interpretation, hypothesizing, and debate, are as follows:

Matzah is to remember leaving Egypt. Naturally, we love that they made sure to grab a snack before **"Rockin' Down the Highway."** ♪

Bitter herbs are because the lives of Jews in Egypt were embittered, so in solidarity we eat a slice of raw horseradish root in between two small pieces of matzah called a Hillel sandwich. Invented by first-century rabbi Hillel the Elder, Seder-goers have flamed their palates, and cleared up any congestion, ever since.

Salt water is for the **"Lonely Teardrops"** of the Jews (and Jackie Wilson, who died at forty-nine). And for everyone who is **"Crying"** like Roy Orbison at the Seder table because they just chewed raw horseradish.

We lean because we are free, and free people may lean as they like.

Got More Questions?

After the Four Questions, some folks make a tradition of asking more questions. These can be about the holiday, current events, or anything that rouses you and engages the others at the Seder. If you're pondering more expansive themes, you can always borrow a song that asks a big question in its title, like Marvin Gaye's **"What's Going On,"** ♪ the Flaming Lips' **"Do You Realize??,"** the Pixies' **"Where Is My Mind?,"** or Elvis Costello and the Attractions' **"(What's So Funny 'Bout) Peace, Love and Understanding"** (written by Nick Lowe).

Was Little Richard Jewish?

I am the innovator. I am the originator. I am the emancipator. I am the architect of rock 'n' roll!" proclaimed Little Richard (born Richard Penniman in 1932). The wild, sacred-meets-profane, gender-bending performer whose influence still surges through the genre called himself a lot of things in his eighty-seven years, including Jewish.

In a 1972 BBC interview, Richard explained why he once quit the music business for bible school (throwing thousands of dollars' worth of jewelry into a river to put an exclamation point on his decision). "I went to study religion, the Jewish religion . . . the Sabbath and the Passover feast," he said.

The singer heralded his love of Judaism many times throughout his life, though he was actually a Seventh-Day Adventist. But to honor this rock 'n' roll trailblazer at your Passover feast, feel free to emancipate your "amens" with Little Richard's signature "Woooooo!"

Avadim Hayinu: We Were Slaves

This is recited or sung: We were slaves to Pharaoh in Egypt—now we are free.

עֲבָדִים הָיִינוּ לְפַרְעֹה בְּמִצְרַיִם, וַיּוֹצִיאֵנוּ יְיָ אֱלֹהֵינוּ מִשָּׁם בְּיָד חֲזָקָה וּבִזְרֹעַ נְטוּיָה. וְאִלּוּ לֹא הוֹצִיא הַקָּדוֹשׁ בָּרוּךְ הוּא אֶת אֲבוֹתֵינוּ מִמִּצְרַיִם, הֲרֵי אָנוּ וּבָנֵינוּ וּבְנֵי בָנֵינוּ מְשֻׁעְבָּדִים הָיִינוּ לְפַרְעֹה בְּמִצְרַיִם. וַאֲפִילוּ כֻּלָּנוּ חֲכָמִים כֻּלָּנוּ נְבוֹנִים כֻּלָּנוּ זְקֵנִים כֻּלָּנוּ יוֹדְעִים אֶת הַתּוֹרָה מִצְוָה עָלֵינוּ לְסַפֵּר בִּיצִיאַת מִצְרַיִם. וְכָל הַמַּרְבֶּה לְסַפֵּר בִּיצִיאַת מִצְרַיִם הֲרֵי זֶה מְשֻׁבָּח.

Avadeem hayeenoo lephar'o bemitzra'yeem, va'yo'tzee'anoo Adonoi Elohaynoo mee'sham b'yad chazakah oo've'zro'a netooyah.

Ve'eeloo lo hotzee Hakadosh Baruch Hoo et avotaynoo mee'mitzrayeem, haray anoo oo'vanaynoo oo'vnay vanaynoo m'shoo'badeem hayeenoo lephar'o bemitzra'yeem. Va'afeeloo koolanoo chachameem koolanoo nevoneem koolanoo zekayneem koolanoo yod'eem et ha'Torah mitzvah alaynoo lesapayr bee'tzee'at mitzrayeem. Vechol ha'marbeh lesapayr bee'tzee'at mitzrayeem haray zeh meshoobach.

Madonna's Holiday

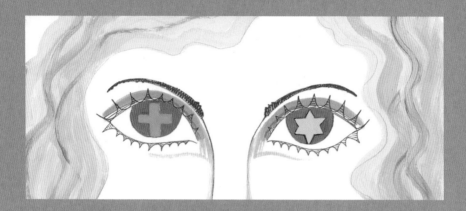

Madonna. Her very name evokes images of not only the Virgin Mary but also the way she (the artist, not Mary) melded Catholic iconography with pop culture. She turned rosary beads into a hot accessory. Her religious upbringing played a huge role in her superstardom, from her song lyrics to the crucifixes with which she adorned herself.

Before she became an icon, though, Madonna found herself singing at a Passover celebration at Chasen's in the presence of some high-level record company executives. "She sang from the Haggadah," according to music honcho Michael Rosenblatt, who discovered Madonna and whose family welcomed her in. "She was the strongest voice in the Rosenblatt family," he adds, laughing.

The future global superstar had traveled to Los Angeles in the spring of 1983 with Rosenblatt, an A&R man for Sire Records at the time. They'd met at Danceteria, the infamous New York City nightclub (where Madonna's character Susan dances with New Jersey yuppie Gary Glass in *Desperately Seeking Susan*), and he immediately saw her potential. Sire signed Madonna and released a couple of dance singles, but Rosenblatt needed money from the Los Angeles–based parent company, Warner Bros., to get her back into the studio to record one more song. He also needed a song that would be a surefire hit to launch her debut album.

Rosenblatt and Madonna stayed at his parents' house, which might seem strange unless you know who his father is—Eddie Rosenblatt, who cofounded and ran Geffen Records for nearly two decades. Eddie was one of the bigwigs who started the Chasen's Passover tradition that drew a group of powerful music movers and shakers, along with Mo Ostin (Jimi Hendrix, Paul Simon, Van Halen), Lenny Waronker (Prince, R.E.M.), and Mickey Rudin (celebrity lawyer for Frank Sinatra, Steely Dan).

"We grew up surrounded by rock stars," Rosenblatt says, recalling the time his parents threw a party for Led Zeppelin guitarist Jimmy Page, and a guy helping them string up lights fell off his ladder when he heard about the guest of honor.

Michael and Madonna arrived in Los Angeles on Passover, and the Rosenblatts took their houseguest to the annual Chasen's Seder. "She was dressed in black with a bunch of crucifixes," Rosenblatt says. "But she was in all the way." Reading the Hebrew transliteration, Madonna started belting out songs. "We went around [the table] and each family would do one of the prayers or sing one of the songs. We knew melodies and started off, but then she took the lead and was singing with all of her heart."

Long before she found Kabbalah, Madonna participated in a Seder with Sire Records' Michael Rosenblatt. "I know that she had fun," he says.

Madonna won everyone over, both at the Seder and the following day at the Warner offices. Rosenblatt got the money to record one more song, and he soon found the material he needed to fully launch the career of the future Material Girl. The song, appropriately enough, was **"Holiday."** ♪

Though Rosenblatt's parents no longer live there, the house is still known as "the house where Madonna stayed."

Rosenblatt's and Madonna's paths would cross again in the 1990s when they both began a journey into Kabbalah, the Jewish mysticism that's said to have been given to Moses along with the Torah on Mount Sinai. "It has some wonderful tools for living," Rosenblatt says of the study and practice of Kabbalah. Introduced to it by her then friend comedian/actress Sandra Bernhard, Madonna chose the Hebrew name Esther; some reflections on her spiritual evolution are heard on her 1998 album *Ray of Light*. The longtime LGBTQIA+ ally became an ally of Israel as well, where she makes frequent visits. With a family of her own, she continues to attend Passover Seders.

We were slaves to Pharaoh in Egypt; now we are free people, and Adonoi our God took us out of there with a strong hand and an outstretched arm. And if the Holy One Blessed Be had not taken our ancestors out of Egypt, then we, and our children, and our children's children would be enslaved to Pharaoh in Egypt. And even if all of us are wise, all of us are intelligent, all of us are elders, all of us know the Torah, it is a commandment for us to tell of the exodus from Egypt. And the more one tells it, the more praiseworthy one is.

"We Were Slaves . . ."

The word "slave" appears in various forms in the bible, in Haggadahs, and in other ancient religious texts of many faiths. We couldn't help but wonder: Were we actually **"Born in Chains,"** 𝄞 as Leonard Cohen sang?

Academic scholars point to evidence that gives us insight into what was happening in the Levant during the late Bronze Age (around 1200 BCE), the period in which the Book of Exodus is set. The pharaohs of that era—Seti I and his son, Ramses II—oversaw a vast military expansion, conscripting laborers to build garrison cities that are thought to be the biblical cities Ramses and Pithom. Egypt was also a Mediterranean hub, attracting visitors on business and migrants from drought- and famine-ravaged lands. Those who stayed tended to assimilate in a generation or two, as immigrants have been doing ever since.

However, the Egyptians did make slaves of some of the nation's residents and accepted the import of enslaved human beings. Regional Canaanite leaders (the "mayors") gifted the Egyptian pharaohs with slaves to court their favor, documented in archaeological finds such as the Amarna Letters (which, incidentally, are clay tablets). Numerous records have been unearthed that reference Semitic immigrant workers in Egypt who may have left because of the pharaohs' harsh labor policies. There's no evidence of a mass migration from Egypt (the Bible calls it "around six hundred thousand"), which may be because the pharaoh did not relish the thought of admitting defeat on the record. There are, however, documents from that era revealing a smaller-scale exodus of people who'd been detained there and who wanted out.

So, we were slaves in Egypt. We're not slaves now, though we may be subjugated by debt, addiction, injustice, or ill health. Slavery continues to exist around the globe in various forms, including human trafficking. We use the word during the Seder not to compare our inherited trauma with anyone else's but rather to consider the nature of freedom—past, present, and future—both metaphorically and literally, as well as the things we can do to improve our world.

The Four Children, or How to Welcome Anyone to Your Seder

The story of the exodus from Egypt includes a mention of four mythological kids. They represent different types of folks with varied levels of knowledge about the holiday and its traditions: the wise, the wicked, the simple, and the one who doesn't know how to ask. Each one poses their own question about the Seder.

The Wise Child is scholarly and metaphysical. "Why do we say these prayers, tell this story, and eat these foods on Passover?" they ask. We tell them, "It's because of what God did for us by bringing us out of Egypt."

The Wicked Child is a rebel—they say, "Why do 'you' do these things on Passover?" instead of "we." Since they've removed themselves from the community, the answer to their question is slightly different: "It's because of what God did for me."

The Simple Child asks a simple question: "What is all this?" They're not sure why we gather on this night. They get a primer on the exodus, and perhaps a homework assignment to watch *The Prince of Egypt*.

The Child Who Doesn't Know How to Ask could be a very young child, or someone who might be afraid to speak up, or who might be uninterested in learning about Passover. Try to engage this person as best you can with relatable stories.

Of course, people are not just one thing. All of us are wise, wicked, simple, and quiet at different times. The Four Children signify that all sorts of folks with all sorts of viewpoints are welcome at the Seder.

Telling the story of Passover may be detailed or philosophical, heavy or light, gory or sanguine, but most likely it will be a combination of these approaches.

The Four Children (Reimagined)

Since this is *The Rock 'n' Roll Haggadah*, we've reimagined the Four Children as the musicians we felt most closely resembled them:

The Wise Child: Bob Dylan

He's rock 'n' roll's sage, its mystic, and one of its most spiritual practitioners. Sure, he checked out of Judaism, but then he checked back in, a subject of endless conjecture by fans and critics. No one comes close to Robert Zimmerman, the artist known as Bob Dylan, rock's first Nobel Prize–winning lyricist, to represent the Wise Child.

Though enigmatically pan-religious, Dylan has made many public expressions of observing Judaism, even around the time of his "Christian era." He hung with the Lubavitcher Rebbe Menachem Schneerson and studied Torah with other rabbis and scholars. He held his son Jesse's bar mitzvah at the Western Wall in Jerusalem. He played "Hava Nagila" on harmonica for the twenty-fifth annual Chabad telethon, jamming with son-in-law Peter Himmelman and actor Harry Dean Stanton, all in yarmulkes; the trio billed themselves as Chopped Liver. And his controversial song "Neighborhood Bully," on the 1983 album *Infidels*, is practically a parable of Jewish exile.

The Wicked Child: Perry Farrell

The perilously arty Perry Farrell was once known as Peretz Bernstein, a kid expelled from Hebrew school for being so much tsuris (Yiddish for "trouble"). Farrell made an unholy, indelible mark on music, founding the bands Jane's Addiction and Porno for Pyros, forever changing rock's landscape with the Lollapalooza festival, and embarking on a solo career with Kabbalah-inspired lyrics. He struggled with drug addiction and credits reconnecting with Judaism—and the teachings of Rebbe Schneerson—as part of what helped him get clean, but he still sways wickedly; for the City Winery's Downtown Seders, Farrell recorded a music video of "Dayenu," a percolating jam of him singing and dancing, set to a backdrop of some of the juicier scenes from *The Ten Commandments*.

The Simple Child: Joey Ramone

The simplicity of the Ramones was their genius. The simplicity of song, stripping 1960s pop music down to its bare chords and playing it at warp speed without losing the integrity of the melody. The simple uniform: black leather jacket, black T-shirt, ripped blue jeans. Four dudes, no relation, one last name. That's as simple as it gets. They wrote songs about being teenage dolts. Their late, great singer Joey Ramone sometimes played a simpleton in popular culture, as he did in the movie *Rock 'n' Roll High School*. Born Jeffrey Hyman, a nice Jewish boy from Queens, New York, he was more complicated in real life. The gangly front man suffered from crippling OCD. He was an avid stock market investor who loved watching CNBC. He also loved strolling around his adopted neighborhood, New York City's East Village. Should you ever find yourself there and yearning for the simplicity of the iconic rocker's persona, head to the corner of Bowery and East Second Street, right near the site of CBGB, the club that launched the Ramones and so many other bands. Look up at the street sign: you'll be standing at Joey Ramone Place.

4

The Child Who Doesn't Know How to Ask: Geddy Lee

Okay, we're fairly certain that singer/bassist Geddy Lee knows how to ask a question. He's represented here for calling himself a "Jewish atheist," distancing himself from religion.

One-third of the band Rush, a Canadian prog-rock power trio with radio hits, millions of albums sold, and a fiercely devoted fan base, he was born Gary Lee Weinrib. His stage name is a tribute to his mother, Mary (Manya). A Polish émigré who landed in Toronto after surviving the Holocaust, her heavy accent made "Gary" sound like "Geddy." She and Lee's father were imprisoned in Europe's most notorious concentration camps. Both were sent to Auschwitz; Morris Weinrib was then moved to Dachau, while Mary endured Bergen-Belsen.

Though the couple gave their kids a Jewish education and Mary vigilantly hosted Passover and other high holy days, Judaism remained a minor part of Lee's life. His parents' experiences, however, left a deep mark on him, making their way into dystopian Rush songs such as **"Red Sector A"** (written by Rush drummer Neil Peart after Lee told him about Mary and Morris's time in the camps), as well as "Grace to Grace" from Lee's 2000 solo album.

Strangers in a Strange Land

Abraham knew it.

The patriarch of the Jewish people was told by God that his children would be "strangers in a land not their own for four hundred years." Sure enough, the Israelites left Canaan (modern-day Israel, more or less) because of famine and traveled to Egypt. We prospered and became enmeshed in the society, culture, business, and politics of our adopted country, becoming "a mighty nation."

The first Israelite to ascend to the heights of power in Egypt was one of Abraham's great-grandsons. Joseph—yes, he of the Amazing Technicolor Dreamcoat, the Canaanite and best-loved son of the patriarch Jacob—was put in charge of all of Egypt by the pharaoh at the time.

As a young man, however, Joseph found himself in the pits. Jealous of Jacob's affection for him, his eleven brothers tossed him into a hole in the ground, and like Slash's Snakepit, they walked away thinking **"Ain't Life Grand."** They planned to kill him but sold him into slavery in exchange for silver instead. The brothers tore up his Jimi Hendrix–worthy coat of many colors and dipped it in goat's blood to convince Jacob that his chosen son was dead.

From there, Joseph was taken to Egypt and given to Potiphar, the pharaoh's captain of the guard. Mrs. Potiphar was drawn to the handsome young Canaanite, deciding he was her **"Magic Man."** 🎵 But Joseph listened to his Heart and said, **"Don't Do Me Like That."** Mrs. P was furious and had him sent to prison. He later landed in the pharaoh's orbit for his extraordinary ability to interpret subconscious stories when the Egyptian ruler was being tormented by the **"Dream Police."** 🎵 Eventually, Joseph was promoted to the highest rank, answering only to Pharaoh himself.

When a famine struck Canaan and people began to starve, Joseph's brothers traveled to Egypt to buy grain. They didn't recognize the potentate of the country's food supply as the little brother they'd cast away, but Joseph recognized them. After some assays, he revealed his identity to them, and they begged his forgiveness. Joseph accepted **"All Apologies,"** 🎵 inviting his brothers to bring their families to the relative Nirvana of Egypt to live and farm.

Upon Joseph's overture, Jacob led the Israelites to Egypt, bringing a posse of seventy. The pharaoh gave them the land of Goshen, a particularly fecund section of the country by the Nile Delta with rich soil for farming. The Israelites flourished in Goshen over generations, and seventy people turned into hundreds, then thousands, then hundreds of thousands—"a mighty nation."

Eventually, a pharaoh unfamiliar with Joseph and the many good things he did as a ruler of Egypt took notice of the large Jewish population in his midst and decided to crush us. This pharaoh claimed to fear that if another nation were to invade Egypt, the Jewish people would join up with the other side, even though we'd been settled there for centuries. Yes, it sounds bogus to us, too.

Every ritual we conduct tonight, every symbolic food we eat and word we utter, every blessing we say, it's all to commemorate what happens after this moment. Because even though it begins here, it doesn't end here. This cycle of welcoming Jews, watching us prosper, then trying to extinguish us has played out all over the world for thousands of years. Somehow, though, we are still here.

Vehi She'amda

Vehi She'amda explains why we're still here—a divine covenant.

Lift up your wine and sing or recite:

וְהִיא שֶׁעָמְדָה לַאֲבוֹתֵינוּ וְלָנוּ. שֶׁלֹּא אֶחָד בִּלְבָד עָמַד עָלֵינוּ לְכַלּוֹתֵנוּ, אֶלָּא שֶׁבְּכָל דּוֹר וָדוֹר עוֹמְדִים עָלֵינוּ לְכַלּוֹתֵנוּ, וְהַקָּדוֹשׁ בָּרוּךְ הוּא מַצִּילֵנוּ מִיָּדָם.

V'hee she-am'dah la-avotaynoo v'lanoo.

Shelo echad bilvad amad alaynoo l'chalotaynoo.

Ela sheb'chol dor vador om'deem alaynoo l'chalotaynoo,

v'HaKadosh Baruch Hoo matzee'laynoo mee-yadam.

And it is this that has stood for our ancestors and for us; that not only one [person or nation] has stood against us to destroy us, but rather in each generation, they stand against us to destroy us, but the Holy One, blessed be, rescues us from their hand.

PUT THE WINE BACK DOWN
ON THE TABLE.

A New Pharaoh Rises

To deal with the Israelites, Pharaoh began to oppress us, severely restricting our freedoms, imposing heavy taxes on us, and forcing us into enslavement. He decided to be the **"King of Pain"** and assigned taskmasters to Police us:

And the Egyptians made the children of Israel serve with rigor:

And they made their lives bitter with hard bondage, in mortar, and in brick, and in all manner of service in the field: all their service, wherein they made them serve, was with rigor.

Sound familiar? The Holocaust comes to mind, but this has happened repeatedly throughout the world to Jews since time immemorial.

Written in the Stars

A surprising number of world leaders have consulted with astrologers (Alexander the Great, Charles de Gaulle, Hitler, Eva Perón, and Ronald Reagan among them), and Pharaoh did, too.

Pharaoh's astrologers looked at **"A Sky Full of Stars"** 🎵 and appealed to his already heightened fears, reporting that a **"New Messiah"** would be born on the 7th of Adar who would grow up to lead the Jewish people in a revolt against the king. Well, wouldn't you know it, Moses was born on that day, which makes him a Pisces. He was reported to be an extraordinarily good-looking baby, with a profound aura.

In order to prevent this astrological prediction from coming to pass, and to control the Israelite population, Pharaoh ordered the Hebrew midwives to drown newborn boys in the Nile. Moses's mother, Yocheved, hid him as best she could. By the time he was three months old, he was too big to conceal, so she took **"Action"** to protect her Sweet baby. She waterproofed a basket, placed him in it, and hid him in the reeds along the bank of the Nile in an attempt to save his life. Yocheved couldn't bear to see what happened after that, but Moses's sister, Miriam, kept an eye on the floating infant.

"Hot Child in the City"

One hot day, Egyptian princess Bithiah told her ladies-in-waiting, **"Take Me to the River,"** 𝄞 where they could all try to be as cool as Al Green. They spotted baby Moses in his basket. Bithiah thought he was supernaturally beautiful; she was instantly smitten and decided to save him. Though he was wailing **"The Weeping Song,"** she could tell he wasn't a Bad Seed. She had some of her bevy attempt to nurse Moses, but he rejected them and kept on crying. Miriam emerged from the reeds and offered to bring a Hebrew midwife to care for the foundling, and she did—their mom, Yocheved.

Point to the cup of water on the table and say:

"This is Miriam's Cup. We place this cup of water on our Seder table to honor Miriam," along with all the "sheroics" in the Book of Exodus.

The Hebrew midwives (represented by Shiphrah and Puah) risk their own lives by not following Pharaoh's orders. Yocheved defies Pharaoh by hiding Moses. Bithiah rescues Moses at her own peril, correctly identifying him as a Hebrew foundling whose family was desperate to save him. She brings him into the palace, rebelling against her own father, and raising him with love as if he were her own. When the Israelites flee Egypt, Bithiah goes with them, giving up the worship of idols and converting to Judaism. When they all reach Mount Sinai, it's the women who keep the faith, refusing to pray to the golden calf. Throughout the Exodus story, women ensure the survival of the Jewish people.

Miriam, like her brothers Moses and Aaron, displays bravery and leadership with a touch of the divine. From the banks of the Nile to her awe at the parting of the Red Sea, Miriam connects with water. During the Israelites' forty-year exile, they draw water from what was known in legend as Miriam's Well—a rock that rolls along with them through the desert and becomes a miraculous Oasis whenever they need hydration—actual rock 'n' roll!

A Stranger in Both Lands

Moses grows up in a unique position, with all the perks of royalty yet connected by blood to his marginalized tribe. It's not clear exactly when he discovers his Jewish identity. After all, Bithiah says she calls him Moses ("to draw out") because she pulled him from the river, and he spends the first couple of years of his life being raised and nursed by his birth mother, Yocheved.

But a pivotal event in his life makes it clear to us, if not to Moses himself, that when you are of two worlds, you're bound to become an OutKast in both. Dropping by Goshen just to say, **"Hey Ya!"** 🎵 to his peeps, he stumbles upon an Egyptian taskmaster beating an Israelite nearly to death. Whether he felt a kinship toward the beaten man, a sense of justice, or both, Moses slays and buries the would-be slayer. He goes back the next day and, upon hearing two Israelites arguing, tries to intervene. The men both turn on him, revealing that they saw him kill the Egyptian and wonder if he'll do the same to them. Afraid of repercussions, and feeling betrayed by people he believed he was helping, Moses decides he was **"Born to Run."** 🎵 He flees from Egypt and lands in Midian, is taken in by Jethro the Midianite, and eventually marries Jethro's daughter, Zipporah. They name their first child Gershom, which means "a stranger there."

"You Should See Me in a Crown"

It should be noted that Moses is eighty years old when he confronts Pharaoh, yet when it comes to public speaking, he's more reticent than Billie Eilish. He doesn't say much in the Book of Exodus and refers to himself as "slow of speech and tongue."

A well-loved legend in the Midrash offers one explanation of this. Moses was such a mesmerizing baby that the royal family loved to interact with him. One day, while Pharaoh was holding him, he reached up, pulled off the ruler's crown, and placed it on his own head. This was considered a sign by the palace flunkies that Moses would one day usurp Pharaoh's power. Instead of talking with the Queen, Pharaoh asked this **"Chain of Fools"** what to do. They figured that **"Everybody Wants to Rule the World,"** so they decided to put tearless, fearless Moses to the test. They placed the little lad between a bowl of gold and a bowl of glowing coals to see if he was just a tot who was drawn to things that **"Shine"** 🎵 or a usurper who would one day rise up against Pharaoh and unite the Jewish people as a Collective Soul. Moses started to go for the gold, but the Angel Gabriel pushed his hand into the "White Hot" coals. He recoiled, putting his hand and a chunk of coal into his mouth and burning his tongue, hence the lifelong disability.

"I'm Burning for You"

While shepherding a flock for Jethro at Mount Horeb, Moses experiences another pivotal moment in his life. He sees the **"Burning Bush,"** and though electronics are millennia away, his Radiohead tunes in a voice. It's the voice of God, telling Moses to take off his sandals, as he's standing on **"Holy Ground."** 🎶

God tasks Moses with confronting Pharaoh to release the Jewish people in His name, even while warning the prince-turned-shepherd that the king's heart would be hardened to the plight of the Israelites. He teaches Moses a few tricks to **"Prove It All Night"** like a Boss. Moses learns to turn a stick into a snake, the Alanis Morissette **"Hand in My Pocket"** leprosy cure (isn't it **"Ironic"**? Take it out and you're cured!), and the positively biblical Bon Jovi **"Blood in the Water"** magic.

Throughout this encounter, Moses is hesitant, as he was oratorically challenged (see the "You Should See Me in a Crown" sidebar) and didn't think he could persuade Pharaoh to let his people go. God instructs him to collect his brother Aaron as a spokesman and take his **"Trick Bag"** 🎶 to the King (and his Earls).

The letters יהוה (yud-hey-vav-hey) form a name for God so sacred that Jews have been prohibited from saying it aloud for millennia. Known as the Tetragrammaton, they appear in Jewish and non-Jewish texts and may be displayed in houses of worship. They are considered by some to have mystical powers.

Alanis Morissette Uncovers Her Jewish Roots

You live, **"You Learn,"** 🎵 Alanis Morissette sang on *Jagged Little Pill*, her multiplatinum, five-time Grammy-winning 1995 album. Morissette's life imitated art just a few years later when the singer/songwriter learned that she's Jewish.

Morissette's mother, Georgia Feuerstein, spent her early life in Hungary, born to Holocaust survivors. In the 1950s, the extended family escaped and immigrated to Canada, where Morissette grew up. The trauma they experienced was more than they could bear, though; they never spoke of it around Morissette and her twin brother, Wade.

"I think there was a terror that is in their bones and they were being protective of us in just not wanting antisemitism," she says.

It was Morissette's grandmother Nadinia who eventually told her of the family history, because Alanis kept asking. "I wouldn't let it go," she says.

Imre Feuerstein, Morissette's grandfather, had survived Nazi genocide and the Soviet invasion of Hungary. His two brothers, Gyorgy and Sandor, were not as lucky. They disappeared during the Holocaust, their fate unknown until Morissette appeared on PBS's *Finding Your Roots* in 2024.

On the program, host Henry Louis Gates Jr. found documents at the Holocaust Museum in Washington, DC, revealing that both men died "in the slave labor army sent to Russia." Red Cross files showed that Imre kept searching for his brothers, never giving up hope.

Morissette was blown away by the show's big reveals and expressed pride in her Jewish identity. "I feel welcomed into a community that I always had a crush on," she says. "I've always had a crush on Judaism, and I would just show up at Passover and at Seder. Now I know why. [It was like,] come home."

Let My People Go

Moses and Aaron confront Pharaoh, saying, **"People Got to Be Free!"** 𝄞 Pharaoh says, **"I Won't Back Down,"** and Moses tells him he's being Petty. The King calls the Israelites **"Lazy Bones,"** and he instructs the taskmasters to make them work even harder.

Moses and Aaron go back to God, who assures them He's no Def Leppard—he hears the cries of the Jewish people and remembers his **"Promises"** to Abraham, Isaac, and Jacob. God sends the **"Brothers in Arms"** back to Pharaoh. This time, when they bust out the **"Strange Magic"** 𝄞 that Moses learned at the burning bush, Pharaoh commands his conjurers to perform the same tricks! Not to be outdone, Aaron's stick becomes a snake that swallows up all the sorcerers' snakes.

This is starting to sound sort of *Harry Potter*-ish.

Phast Pharaoh Phacts

Pharaoh wasn't one guy, or even necessarily a guy. King Tut was a pharaoh. So was Cleopatra. Pharaohs were essentially kings, ruling over Egypt in civic, spiritual, and military matters. The pharaoh in the Book of Exodus is never named—he is simply referred to as Pharaoh. Fans of the film *The Prince of Egypt* take note: Pharaoh and Moses were not brothers. That's just Hollywood adding another plotline to an already extraordinary story.

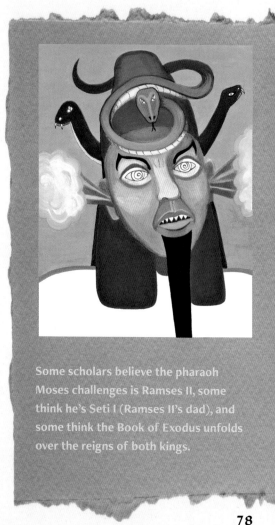

Some scholars believe the pharaoh Moses challenges is Ramses II, some think he's Seti I (Ramses II's dad), and some think the Book of Exodus unfolds over the reigns of both kings.

With a Strong Hand and an Outstretched Arm, with Great Terror, with Signs and Wonders

You wouldn't think it would take a Five Man Electrical Band to see the **"Signs,"** 🎵 but no matter how many times Moses asked, **"Are You Gonna Go My Way"** 🎵, Pharaoh's cruelty toward the enslaved Israelites only grew worse.

This is where magic becomes **"Divine Intervention"** 🎵.

וַיּוֹצִיאֵנוּ יְיָ מִמִּצְרַיִם בְּיָד חֲזָקָה, וּבִזְרֹעַ נְטוּיָה, וּבְמֹרָא גָּדֹל, וּבְאֹתוֹת וּבְמֹפְתִים.

V'yotzee'anoo Adonoi mee'mitzra'yeem b'yad chazakah, oo've'zro'ah netooyah, oo'v'morah gadol, oo'v'otot oo'v'mofteem.

And the Eternal brought us out of Egypt, with a "Strong Hand" and with an outstretched arm, with great terror, and with signs and wonders.

וַיּוֹצִיאֵנוּ יְיָ מִמִּצְרַיִם, לֹא עַל־יְדֵי מַלְאָךְ, וְלֹא עַל־יְדֵי שָׂרָף, וְלֹא עַל־יְדֵי שָׁלִיחַ, אֶלָּא הַקָּדוֹשׁ בָּרוּךְ הוּא בִּכְבוֹדוֹ וּבְעַצְמוֹ.

V'yotzee'anoo Adonoi mee'mitzrayeem. Lo al y'day mal'ach, v'lo al y'day saraf, v'lo al y'day shalee'ach, elah Hakadosh baruch hoo bichvodo oo'v'atzmo.

And Adonoi brought us out of Egypt, not by an angel, nor by a fiery being, nor by an emissary; but the Holy One, blessed be, by his honor and by himself.

שֶׁנֶּאֱמַר: וְעָבַרְתִּי בְאֶרֶץ מִצְרַיִם בַּלַּיְלָה הַזֶּה, וְהִכֵּיתִי כָל־בְּכוֹר בְּאֶרֶץ מִצְרַיִם מֵאָדָם וְעַד בְּהֵמָה, וּבְכָל־אֱלֹהֵי מִצְרַיִם אֶעֱשֶׂה שְׁפָטִים. אֲנִי יְיָ.

She'ne'emar: ve'avartee ve'eretz Mitzrayim ba'lai'lah hazeh, v'hee'kaytee kol bechor be'eretz Mitzrayim may'adam v'ad behayma, oo'vechol elohay Mitzrayim, e'eseh shefateem. Anee Adonoi.

As it is said, "I will pass through the land of Egypt this night and I will strike every firstborn in the land of Egypt, from human to beast; and I will execute judgments against all the gods of Egypt. I am Adonoi."

Susanna Hoffs's "Eternal Flame"

Native Angeleno Susanna Hoffs grew up singing at her family's Passover Seders, but her voice helped propel the Bangles' **"Walk Like an Egyptian"** 𝄞 to the top of the pop charts. With a gaga MTV video and the impossibly catchy girl-group "oh-way-oh" refrain, it was declared *Billboard*'s number one song of 1987. It was sort of an outlier for the group, a literal garage band that formed in 1980 and practiced in Hoffs's parents' Los Angeles garage.

The Bangles crafted literate pop songs, they all sang, and they had impeccable taste in covers, specifically from the 1960s. Columbia Records signed them, and they were elated to be on the label of Bob Dylan and the Byrds. After gliding on the success of "Walk . . . ," they ran a bracing cover of Simon & Garfunkel's **"Hazy Shade of Winter"** that sounded more characteristic of their style—electric guitar riffs, rich harmonies, contemplative lyrics—all the way up the charts to number two.

Hoffs took lead vocals on the Bangles' second and last number one song, **"Eternal Flame,"** which she cowrote with 1980s hitmaker Billy Steinberg (Madonna, Cyndi Lauper). Hoffs told Steinberg about the Bangles' visit to Graceland, Elvis Presley's Memphis compound-turned-tourist attraction. The band noticed that the eternal flame at Elvis's shrine wasn't so eternal—it had been snuffed out in the rain.

Steinberg conjured a different image, one from his childhood synagogue in Palm Springs, California. In every Jewish temple, there's an ark that holds the Torah, and over the ark is an "eternal flame," a light or lamp that never goes out. It's one of the orders the Israelites receive in the Book of Exodus, to keep this eternal flame burning. Through the sacking of our Holy Temples and persecution, its symbolism grew over the millennia.

The original language dictates that the eternal flame continue using pure oil made with crushed olives, but modern sanctuaries tend to differ. Steinberg equates the one he grew up with to a little red Christmas light. He spent countless hours gazing at the light over the ark, pondering its mysteries. Maybe that's why "Eternal Flame" has such a dreamlike quality. Or maybe it's that the song has no drums and no chorus. Or maybe it's Hoffs's quavering vocals. Whatever else it was, it was also the Bangles' 1980s swan song; they embarked upon a nine-year break a few months after its release.

The song "Walk Like an Egyptian" was written by Liam Sternberg, inspired by the sight of his fellow ferry passengers awkwardly disembarking after crossing the English Channel.

The Ten Plagues

The Ten Plagues may be recited together, or the host may lead a call and response with the rest of the guests at the Seder. When each plague is uttered, we remove a bit of wine from our glasses. Use your finger to make ten wine dots on your plate (or napkin), or **"Spill the Wine"** 𝄞 into a bowl like Eric Burdon declaring War:

1

Blood—*Dam* דָּם

2

Frogs—*Tzfardayah* צְפַרְדֵּעַ

3

Lice—*Kinim* כִּנִּים

4

Wild Beasts/Swarms of Insects—*Arov* עָרוֹב

5

Pestilence of Livestock— *Dever* דֶּבֶר

6

Boils—*Sh'cheen* שְׁחִין

7

Hail—*Barad* בָּרָד

8

Locusts—*Arbeh* אַרְבֶּה

9

Darkness—*Choshech* חֹשֶׁךְ

10

Slaying of the Firstborn— *Makat b'chorot* מַכַּת בְּכוֹרוֹת

Between the Devil and the Deep Red Sea

After many reneged promises to let the Jews leave Egypt, Pharaoh finally relents. Then he changes his mind again and sends his cavalry to chase us.

Trapped between the shoreline and the encroaching army, the Israelites separate into four groups. One group wants to plunge into the water. Another thinks they should return to Egypt. The third says "Let's fight them!" And the fourth says "Let's pray."

Moses nixes all their ideas. God tells him that he—Moses—holds the power:

> *Why do you cry out to Me? Speak to the children of*
> *Israel and let them travel. And you raise your staff and*
> *stretch out your hand over the sea and split it . . .*

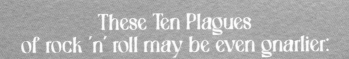

These Ten Plagues
of rock 'n' roll may be even gnarlier:

Taylor Swift,
"Bad Blood"—HEY!

Nonpoint,
"Breaking Skin"

Lou Reed (feat. David
Bowie), "Hop Frog"

Halestorm,
"Apocalyptic"

Pearl Jam,
"Bugs"

Machine Head, "Locust"

The Rolling Stones,
"Beast of Burden"

The Youngbloods,
"Darkness, Darkness"

Metallica,
"Creeping Death"

Foo Fighters,
"For All the Cows"

The waters part. It's a miracle . . . or is it? Scientists have done studies and simulations of winds and waves proving that something like that could've happened, not at the Red Sea but in the eastern Nile Delta. Slogging across its muddy flats, however, is not as awe-inspiring as the story in the Book of **"Exodus."** 🎼 This moment pits not only faith against reason but also Moses's leadership against Pharaoh's autocracy. The Israelites' escape through the temporary divide is as spectacular as the cavalry's destruction. In his song **"Ocean,"** 🎼 Lou Reed describes whatever sea he's thinking about as "mad," which can be said of the Red Sea when Pharaoh's army arrives. The Civil War–era spiritual **"O Mary Don't You Weep,"** which Bruce Springsteen sings on *We Shall Overcome: The Seeger Sessions*, describes what happened next—they got "drown-ded."

Pour One Out

It's customary to dip or spill wine three more times for "blood, fire, and pillars of smoke," and some add yet another three for "*detzach, adash, b'achav,*" דְּצַ"ךְ עֲדַ"שׁ בְּאַחַ"ב , a mnemonic device for all ten plagues created by second-century Rabbi Yehuda. The number sixteen has additional symbolic and mystical meaning, including a Midrash passage describing the **"Sword of God"** as having sixteen edges, and the sixteen-word song "Kadesh Urchatz" that names the sections of the Seder.

As is the case with many Jewish customs and laws, there are many interpretations of the spilling of wine during the reading of the Ten Plagues. Some use their forefingers to administer the "plague-to-plate" wine to symbolize the belief of Pharaoh's magicians, who told their king that the plagues were "the finger of God." Some think the "drops" represent how the Ten Plagues are actually small compared with what awaits evildoers when God really gets mad.

One interpretation that's central to Jewish identity, though, is from Proverbs 24:17: "When your enemy has fallen, do not rejoice." As our rabbi explained to us as kids, we're still sad because people died, so our joy is diminished. Anyone who has seen an episode of *Curb Your Enthusiasm*, created by and starring writer/comedian/*Seinfeld* co-creator Larry David, knows that "diminished joy" is a part of a Jewish stereotype . . . and a funny one at that.

The commingling of elation and sorrow ripples throughout Jewish tradition, from the Seder to stomping on a glass at weddings to remember the destruction of the Holy Temples (among other things). It also makes a fine template for rock 'n' roll. Think about songs with upbeat melodies and devastating lyrics, such as Foster the People's **"Pumped Up Kicks"** (school shootings), Bruce Springsteen's **"Born in the U.S.A."** (Vietnam veterans), Nena's **"99 Luftballons"** (nuclear war), Creedence Clearwater Revival's **"Bad Moon Rising"** (a coming apocalypse), and pretty much the entire Clash catalog (**"Spanish Bombs," "Rock the Casbah," "Clampdown"** . . . you get the picture). Jewish lore, plus millennia of persecution, tends to make us not be too loud whether we prevail or fail. Unless, of course, we're singing.

A Band of Evil Angels

Some of Judaism's most famous sages who predate the early ages had "a think" about God and the Ten Plagues, and it made them do math: If God's finger represents ten plagues, then His hand must've brought fifty plagues, which somehow becomes fifty plagues for each finger on His hand—hence two hundred fifty plagues. This is where the Seder departs from the journey out of Egypt and enters philosophical Mishnah territory. We like it for referencing Psalm 78's "band of evil angels":

> He unleashed upon them the fierceness
> of his anger, wrath, and indignation, and
> trouble, a band of evil angels.

But they were not a band, nor were they principally evil. They were, however, dispatched to wreak a **"Symphony of Destruction"** and Megadeth among Pharaoh's army.

It's not so much about the numbers of plagues as it is the concept of good and evil. It's like when Abraham haggles with God over sparing Sodom and Gomorrah in Genesis (the book, not the band) because there might be a few good folks among the debauched masses. Abe asks the Lord to consider not **"Throwing It All Away"** if they can find fifty righteous people, and eventually they negotiate down to ten. (Unleavened bread makes an appearance in that story, too, when the Sodomite Lot whips some up for the angels sent to destroy the place.)

It's a reminder that Judaism isn't just a religion—it's a way of living. The same ancient texts that calculate plagues and ponder divine justice versus human catastrophe also list the best way to go to sleep at night (on your side, with your shoes off, and no food under the bed). You can utilize this knowledge **"Any Way You Want It"** ♪ on your personal Journey through life.

How Cecil B. DeMille Inspired Metallica's Exodus Song

Springtime brings repeated airings of Cecil B. DeMille's 1956 biblical epic, *The Ten Commandments* (his second version of the story; his first was a 1923 silent film that was also a box office hit). For families around the world, viewing the larger-than-life Technicolor classic—all three hours and thirty-nine minutes of it, complete with a ten-minute intermission—is a tradition. Drummer Lars Ulrich's family was one of them.

"I was obsessed with *The Ten Commandments* as a kid," says Ulrich, who spent his childhood in Denmark before moving to California and cofounding the revolutionary metal band Metallica.

For the Ulrichs, the tale of Jews escaping a tyrannical ruler was personal. Ulla Ulrich, Lars's paternal grandmother, was Jewish. When Hitler invaded Denmark in 1940, she and fifteen-year-old son Torben (Lars's dad) fled to Sweden via fishing boat. They were shot at and intercepted by Nazis and sent to a concentration camp at Elsinore. Lars's grandfather, legendary Danish tennis champion Einer Ulrich, supposedly used his notoriety to get them out. Six weeks later, they escaped again and made it to Sweden, where they waited out the rest of the war. When Torben returned to Denmark, he, too, became a tennis champ and was the first to break his father's record of playing seventy-four Davis Cup games (Torben played one hundred one).

Perhaps Metallica fans can thank Lars Ulrich's family background for his intensity. They can certainly thank his grandma for buying him his first drum kit at age twelve.

In another part of the world—Richmond, California, to be exact—high school student and future Metallica axman Kirk Hammett was pushing the limits of guitar playing in his first band, Exodus. Yep, that's right: EXODUS. "I was trying to write something heavier than the bands I was listening to, and that felt like the first time that I'd done it," he says. "Kind of, like, 'Wow, I'm on to something!'"

Metallica formed in 1981, but it wasn't until they were working on their second album, *Ride the Lightning*, that they recycled Hammett's crunching riff in the exodus-inspired song "Creeping Death." The six-and-a-half-minute opus is their second-most-performed live song, and *Guitar World* magazine ranked it as the best song in their nearly four-decade career.

Ulrich, singer/guitarist James Hetfield, and bassist Cliff Burton had gotten a hold of *The Ten Commandments* on video. The three young musicians were engrossed by DeMille's depiction of the Ten Plagues, especially the last plague, which Ulrich describes: "Then this fog appears out of the moon and comes down and starts creeping across the ground, smoke machine style, and everybody who's caught in it falls over and dies on the spot."

Burton (who died when the band's tour bus crashed in 1986) came up with the title "Creeping Death." The song is written from the perspective of the Angel of Death, referencing the havoc caused by the other plagues before he delivers the final death blow to the Egyptians. "If you watch the movie, you can definitely see that it inspired **'Creeping Death,'** says Ulrich. "There's a connection."

Some Metallica fans have Lars Ulrich's face tattooed on their bodies, but the drummer himself has no tattoos.

forty Years in the Desert

After the exodus from Egypt, Moses ascended Mount Sinai to receive the word of God, who was inscribing the Ten Commandments onto stone tablets. Hey, good masonry work takes time! Forty days and forty nights, apparently.

While they waited, some of the folks grew impatient and lost their faith and perhaps their minds. There was no communication, no Drake **"Hotline Bling,"** no ELO **"Telephone Line,"** not even Phoebe Bridgers's **"Smoke Signals."** They began to (Stevie) Wonder why Moses was on **"Higher Ground"** ♪ for so long, and panic set in that they might die in the wilderness. These men implored Moses's brother Aaron to create an idol to worship. To mollify the Band of Heathens, he collected their precious metals to build a **"Golden Calf,"** a symbol of strength related to the Canaanite god El.

The women, however, did not participate in the treachery. These Twisted Sisters said **"We're Not Gonna Take It,"** ♪ holding on to both their treasures and their faith in the God who had freed them.

Ever wonder how, if we were enslaved for so long, we left Egypt with enough gold to create such a monstrosity? In the Book of Exodus, God states:

> *I will make the Egyptians favorably disposed toward [the Hebrews], so that when you leave you will not go empty-handed. Every woman is to ask her neighbor and any woman living in her house for articles of silver and gold and for clothing, which you will put on your sons and daughters.*

Another version is this: after God went full Rage Against the Machine, **"Killing in the Name"** with the tenth plague, Pharaoh and his henchmen wanted the Israelites out of the country fast before any more Egyptians were killed. They told the Jewish Mötley Crüe something like: Reap these riches, bag the bangles, grab this souvenir statue of the Giza Pyramids, and **"Get Out of Here."** So Aaron had plenty of metal to work with.

Scholars have put forth several reasons why Aaron, a spiritual leader in his own right, would waste a Weeknd building **"False Idols."** They've surmised everything from his possible fear that for Moses, being close to God was like a drug and that he was **"Gone for Good,"** or that the Disturbed Israelite men were looking for **"A Reason to Fight"** and might tear him apart if he didn't do what they wanted. Whatever his motive, Aaron made the graven **"Effigy."** Then he ordered a feast prepared for the idolaters to commemorate this new golden god.

Moses was infuriated when he saw the Libertines worshipping the golden calf. He hurled the tablets, with their sacred words written by the finger of God, at the group. Not cool. He had to go back up the mountain and ask God to go **"Over It Again."**

As angry as Moses was, however, his rage in the Book of Exodus pales in comparison to God's, who wanted to end the entire tribe right there at Mount Sinai. Moses pleaded with Him on behalf of the Jewish people, saying **"We Can Work It Out."** And they did. As a consequence, we remained in the wilderness for forty years, until the calf-worshipping generation had died off, before the generations that followed could enter **"The Promised Land."** For his part in the fracas (breaking the original tablets), Moses was never allowed in.

91

While we're at it, here are the Ten Commandments. It should be noted that they are only the first ten of 613 commandments that govern observant Jewish life, so consider them a biblical Bill of Rights.

1. I am the Lord thy God, who brought thee out of the land of Egypt, out of the house of bondage.

2. Thou shalt have no other gods before Me.

3. Thou shalt not take the name of the Lord thy God in vain.

4. Remember the Sabbath day to keep it holy.

5. Honor thy father and thy mother.

6. Thou shalt not murder.

7. Thou shalt not commit adultery.

8. Thou shalt not steal.

9. Thou shalt not bear false witness against thy neighbor.

10. Thou shalt not covet anything that belongs to thy neighbor.

Whether you believe this story is a myth based on historical events, religious doctrine, or you don't believe it at all, there are some commonsense ideas in those commandments, things like don't kill anyone, don't steal stuff, don't lie, and don't covet—that last one seems to cause most of the others to be broken. They're also the basis of countless songs, but here are ten to get you started:

Bob Dylan: "Little Moses" (#1)

Louis Armstrong: "Shadrack" (#2)

The Grateful Dead: "Uncle John's Band" (#3)

Leonard Cohen: "After the Sabbath Prayers" (#4)

Taylor Swift: "The Best Day" (#5)

Queen: "Bohemian Rhapsody" (#6)

Jay-Z: "4:44" (#7)

Jane's Addiction: "Been Caught Stealing" (#8)

Bo Diddley: "Before You Accuse Me" (#9)

Derek and the Dominos: "Layla" (#10)

Representing the other 603, we present the OG—blessed with a deity-like voice, he helped invent rock 'n' roll by blending a bunch of genres and stripping the music down to the basics—Johnny Cash: **"The Ten Commandments."** It appears on Cash's gospel album *The Holy Land*, much of which he and his new bride, June Carter Cash, recorded on-site during their honeymoon pilgrimage to Israel in 1968.

"Whip It Good":
A Persian and Afghan Tradition

During the Jews' forty-year sojourn in the desert, God provided sustenance to keep us alive. Yes, we were being punished, but we weren't being tortured, and people gotta eat! He sent manna, which has been described as a sort of white grain that tasted like "wafers made with honey." **"Manna from Heaven"** has since become a metaphor for anything so delectable that it defies description. At the time, however, the tribe missed the food they'd had in Egypt, which was flavored with **"Green Onions"** ♪. Can you imagine complaining to Almighty because the Cake he sent you every morning wasn't going **"The Distance"**?

To commemorate their audacious love of savories, Persian and Afghan Jewish families have a tradition of swatting at one another with scallions during the singing of "Dayenu." This is particularly fun during the ninth and tenth verses, when manna is mentioned, and during the choruses, which are sung in a lively manner. Passed down through generations, they continue to link "Dayenu" with DEVO as they **"Whip It Good."** ♪

If you have scallions, bust them out now and **"Let It Whip"**!

Dayenu:
It Would Have Been Sufficient

"Dayenu," the most recognizable song from the Seder, gallops through a history of the Jews from bondage in Egypt to the parting of the Red Sea to the building of the first Holy Temple in Jerusalem. Each step along the way, we recognize what God did for us and essentially say, "If he'd only done that, it would have been enough." It's a song of giving thanks, but it also reflects the heart of Jewish endurance. Day (pronounced "dai") is the Hebrew word for "enough," and enu is "to us." It would've been enough for us!

Like if the Rolling Stones had quit after *Some Girls*—dayenu. If U2 stopped winning Grammys after *The Joshua Tree*—dayenu. If God Is My Co-Pilot had only covered Israel's national anthem, **"Hatikvah,"** on their album *Mir Shlufn Nisht* (*I Don't Sleep*) and not also recorded "Dayen . . ." Never mind, we like that one.

Some folks sing the first verse and chorus together in Hebrew, then read the English verses as a call-and-response: for each line read by the host, everyone at the table responds with a rousing "Dayenu!" Seder pros can sing or recite the whole song in Hebrew and read the English afterward for the non–Hebrew speakers.

Verse:

אִלּוּ הוֹצִיאָנוּ מִמִּצְרַיִם, דַּיֵּנוּ.

Eeloo ho'tzee, ho'tzee'anoo,
ho'tzee'anoo mee-Mitz-ra-yim

Mee-Mitz-ra-yim ho'tzee'anoo
dai'yay'noo

Chorus:

Dai-dai-yay-noo,
Dai-dai-yay-noo,
Dai-dai-yay-noo,
Dai-yay-oo, dai-yay-noo!

אִלּוּ הוֹצִיאָנוּ מִמִּצְרַיִם וְלֹא עָשָׂה בָהֶם שְׁפָטִים,
דַּיֵּנוּ.

Eeloo hotzee'anoo mee'mitzra'yim
v'lo asah bahem sh'fatim,
dai'yay'noo
(Chorus)

אִלּוּ עָשָׂה בָהֶם שְׁפָטִים וְלֹא עָשָׂה בֵאלֹהֵיהֶם, דַּיֵּנוּ.

Eelu asah vahem sh'fatim
v'lo asah vay'lo'hay'hem,
dai'yay'noo
(Chorus)

אִלּוּ עָשָׂה בֵאלֹהֵיהֶם וְלֹא הָרַג אֶת בְּכוֹרֵיהֶם, דַּיֵּנוּ.

Eelu asah vay'lo'hay'hem
v'lo harag et b'cho'ray'hem,
dai'yay'noo
(Chorus)

אִלּוּ הָרַג אֶת בְּכוֹרֵיהֶם וְלֹא נָתַן לָנוּ אֶת מָמוֹנָם,
דַּיֵּנוּ.

Eelu harag et b'cho'ray'hem
v'lo natan la'noo et ma'monam,
dai'yay'noo
(Chorus)

אִלּוּ נָתַן לָנוּ אֶת מָמוֹנָם וְלֹא קָרַע לָנוּ אֶת הַיָּם,
דַּיֵּנוּ.

Eelu natan lanoo et ma'monam
v'lo kara lanoo et hayam,
dai'yay'noo
(Chorus)

אִלּוּ קָרַע לָנוּ אֶת הַיָּם וְלֹא הֶעֱבִירָנוּ בְּתוֹכוֹ
בֶּחָרָבָה, דַּיֵּנוּ.

Eelu kara lanoo et ha'yam
v'lo he'eh'veeranoo b'tocho
becharavah,
dai'yay'noo
(Chorus)

אִלּוּ הֶעֱבִירָנוּ בְּתוֹכוֹ בֶּחָרָבָה וְלֹא שִׁקַּע צָרֵינוּ
בְּתוֹכוֹ, דַּיֵּנוּ.

Ee'loo he'eh'vee'ranoo b'tocho
becharavah
v'lo sheeka tzaraynoo b'tocho,
dai'yay'noo
(Chorus)

אִלּוּ שִׁקַּע צָרֵינוּ בְּתוֹכוֹ וְלֹא סִפֵּק צָרְכֵּנוּ בַּמִּדְבָּר
אַרְבָּעִים שָׁנָה, דַּיֵּנוּ.

Eelu sheeka tzaraynoo b'tocho
v'lo see'payk tzor'kaynoo bamidbar
arba'eem shana,
dai'yay'nu
(Chorus)

אִלּוּ סִפֵּק צָרְכֵּנוּ בַּמִּדְבָּר אַרְבָּעִים שָׁנָה וְלֹא
הֶאֱכִילָנוּ אֶת הַמָּן, דַּיֵּנוּ.

Ee'loo see'payk tzor'kaynoo bamidbar arba'eem shana
v'lo he'eh'cheelanoo et haman,
dai'yay'noo
(Chorus)

אִלּוּ הֶאֱכִילָנוּ אֶת הַמָּן וְלֹא נָתַן לָנוּ אֶת הַשַּׁבָּת, דַּיֵּנוּ.

Ee'loo he'eh'chee'lanoo et haman
v'lo natan lanoo et ha-Shabbat,
dai'yay'noo
(Chorus)

אִלּוּ נָתַן לָנוּ אֶת הַשַּׁבָּת וְלֹא קֵרְבָנוּ לִפְנֵי הַר סִינַי, דַּיֵּנוּ.

Ee'loo natan lanoo et ha-Shabbat
v'lo kayr'vanoo lifnay har Sinai,
dai'yay'noo
(Chorus)

אִלּוּ קֵרְבָנוּ לִפְנֵי הַר סִינַי וְלֹא נָתַן לָנוּ אֶת הַתּוֹרָה. דַּיֵּנוּ.

Ee'loo kayr'vanoo lif'nay har see'nai
v'lo natan lanoo et ha-Torah,

dai'yay'noo
(Chorus)

אִלּוּ נָתַן לָנוּ אֶת הַתּוֹרָה וְלֹא הִכְנִיסָנוּ לְאֶרֶץ יִשְׂרָאֵל, דַּיֵּנוּ.

Ee'loo natan la'noo et ha-Torah
v'lo hich'nee'sanoo l'eretz yisra'ayl,
dai'yay'noo
(Chorus)

אִלּוּ הִכְנִיסָנוּ לְאֶרֶץ יִשְׂרָאֵל וְלֹא בָנָה לָנוּ אֶת בֵּית הַבְּחִירָה, דַּיֵּנוּ.

Ee'loo hich'nee'sanoo l'eretz yisra'ayl
v'lo vanah lanoo et beit habecheera,
dai'yay'noo

(Chorus)

Call-and-response:

If He had brought us out from Egypt
and had not carried out judgments
against them—dayenu!

If He had carried out judgments
against them and not against their
idols—dayenu!

If He had destroyed their idols
and had not smitten their
firstborn—dayenu!

If He had smitten their firstborn and had not given us their
wealth—dayenu!

If He had given us their wealth and
had not split the sea for us—dayenu!

If He had split the sea for us and
had not taken us through it on dry
land—dayenu!

If He had taken us through the sea
on dry land and had not drowned our
oppressors in it—dayenu!

If He had drowned our oppressors in
it and had not supplied our needs in
the desert for forty years—dayenu!

If He had supplied our needs in the
desert for forty years and had not
fed us manna—dayenu!

If He had fed us manna and had not
given us the Shabbat—dayenu!

If He had given us the Shabbat and
had not brought us before Mount
Sinai—dayenu!

If He had brought us before Mount
Sinai and had not given us the
Torah—dayenu!

If He had given us the Torah and
had not brought us into the land of
Israel—dayenu!

If He had brought us into the land of
Israel and not built for us the Holy
Temple—dayenu!

A Very Grateful Dead Seder

For many years, a group of nomads follow a bearded man. He channels the mystical words and vivid imagery of an enigmatic being.

Moses guiding us through the desert? Or Jerry Garcia enrapturing fans with the words of Grateful Dead lyricist Robert Hunter?

Both! Many have pondered the large number of Jews who comprise jam band fans, particularly "Deadheads," fervent followers of the Grateful Dead. A small subsect calls themselves "Jews for Jerry," as in singer/guitarist Jerry Garcia—the nine-fingered virtuoso who couldn't flip you off with his right hand due to a childhood ax-ident.

Perhaps the appeal resides in the sense of belonging and acceptance within a community. Or the way the Grateful Dead catalog is subject to seemingly limitless interpretations, like Judaism and Jewish traditions. Certainly, the euphoric experience of rock fans singing along with songs they've heard countless times can mirror a temple congregation on holy days. And if you've ever attended a religious Jewish service, you've witnessed the "shuckle" shared by congregants and concertgoers—the back-and-forth swaying motion done when a song or prayer moves them.

A founding member of the Grateful Dead, bassist Phil Lesh took notice of the many Jewish people among the group's flock. For several years, he held Seders at Terrapin Crossroads, his San Rafael, California, music venue. Though not Jewish himself—that lone distinction belongs to the Dead's percussionist Mickey Hart (aka Long Island, New York's own Michael Hartman)—Lesh narrated the Passover story and led performances for hundreds of happy Deadheads. He enlisted cantorial soloist Jeannette Ferber to help organize the events and sing with the band. Though the club closed permanently in 2021, Ferber explains the significance of the Seders held there: *Terrapin Crossroads was a very special place. When Phil opened the music venue and restaurant, it quickly attracted a community of Deadhead regulars. There was a nearly constant flow of ticketed shows in the venue, called the Grate Room, and free shows in the bar/restaurant daily. For most holidays, secular and not, you could count on there being something going on at Terrapin, and since they really wanted it to be an inclusive place, some Jewish holidays were included in this. That's how I ended up getting to sing there and be a part of the epic annual Terrapin Nation Passover Seders from 2014 to 2019. I had been serving as a cantorial soloist for a Jewish Renewal community in Berkeley for a number of years, where we have traditions such as working [Dylan's] "Knocking on Heaven's Door" into "Avinu Malkeinu" during high holiday services, so mixing rock 'n' roll and Judaism already made perfect sense to me!*

We put together a Grateful Dead–themed Haggadah, gave Terrapin's chef a long list of food to make (and guidelines about what not to make), and assembled a crew of musicians to play a post-meal, Passover-themed set of music.

Various members of the community would take on leading parts of the Seder. Phil would usually help light the candles and read the story of the exodus. A deeply spiritual man, Phil genuinely appreciated the power of ritual and community. We also had a lot of fun commiserating during the meal. It was very surreal to get to celebrate Passover with a music icon!

The post-Seder concert was always a highlight of the event. A great crew of Jewish musicians from the Bay Area Dead scene would play alongside Phil, including Dan Lebowitz, Ross James, Ezra Lipp, Scott Law, Brian Rashap, Scott Guberman, and myself. It was always fun picking out Grateful Dead and Jerry Garcia Band songs that had a theme or lyrics that connected to Passover, like **"Waiting for a Miracle,"** 🎼 **"Promised Land,"** **"Touch of Grey,"** and **"Ain't No Bread in the Breadbox."** We would also do songs like Bob Marley's **"Exodus,"** Leonard Cohen's **"Hallelujah,"** and [the African American spiritual] **"Go Down, Moses."** I always loved singing [Kris Kristofferson's] **"Me and Bobby McGee"** [for its lyrics about freedom].

There was something extra special about playing a rock 'n' roll show right after experiencing such an ancient ritual. It was deeply meaningful to be able to honor our ancestors as well as ourselves, by integrating the music we love into our Passover celebration.

One of the most touching things for me was that so many folks who came to the Seders were Jews that had not celebrated Passover or other Jewish holidays in a long time. It became very clear to me how important it is for people to be able to celebrate these kinds of traditions in a way that feels relevant and personally meaningful to them.

The first year we did the Seder, we had around one hundred twenty-five people in the Grate Room. By the final year, because of how popular it had become, the event was held in Terrapin's newer outside venue space, where we held two nights of Seders with four hundred attendees each night.

I'll always cherish the memories of the Seders we were lucky enough to have there. Although it's sad that Terrapin is no longer open, many of us who were involved with the Seders there have continued the tradition. We did a couple of them virtually on Zoom during the pandemic (Phil attended the 2020 Seder), and then last year we joyously reconvened in person once again. As the lyrics in **"Touch of Grey"** 🎼 say: "We will get by. We will survive!"

The Big Three

In rock 'n' roll, the Big Three may be any of the following:

🎼 A Merseybeat group that shared a manager (Jewish Liverpudlian Brian Epstein) with the Beatles.

🎼 A band featuring "Mama" Cass Elliot (born Ellen Naomi Cohen) before the Mamas and the Papas.

🎼 The "holy trinity" of guitar, bass, and drums.

Passover's Big Three come from Rabban Gamliel, a descendant of Hillel and a rabbinic sage at the time of the destruction of the Second Temple in Jerusalem (70 CE). He named the paschal lamb, matzah, and maror, and stated that anyone who doesn't explain the significance of those three has not fulfilled their Passover duty.

Why go to the trouble of saying this when we've already gone to all the trouble of having a Seder? Because **"It's Not Enough"** 🎼 just to Thunder through the rituals: We are obligated to discuss these things as well. This underscores the importance of the oral tradition as a factor in keeping Judaism alive, and it has worked for thousands of years.

THE SEDER HOST DOES
AND SAYS THE FOLLOWING.

Lift the shank bone and say:

This is the paschal lamb our ancestors ate when the Holy Temples stood, a Passover sacrifice made to the Almighty who "passed over" our houses in Egypt on the night of the tenth plague.

Lift the matzahs and say:

This is the unleavened bread, which baked on the backs of our ancestors as they were brought forth from Egypt, because they had no time to let it rise.

Lift the bitter herb and say:

This bitter herb is eaten because the Egyptians embittered the lives of our ancestors with hard labor, with bricks and mortar and in the field.

בְּכָל דּוֹר וָדוֹר חַיָּב אָדָם לִרְאוֹת אֶת עַצְמוֹ כְּאִלּוּ הוּא יָצָא מִמִּצְרָיִם.

B'chol dor va dor cha'yav ah'dam lir'ot et atzmo ke'eeloo hoo yatza mee'mitz'ra'yim.

In every generation, a person is obligated to regard oneself as if they went out of Egypt.

Hallel—Part 1

Psalms 113–18 are known collectively as Hallel, and they're recited in various forms at several Jewish holidays, including Pesach (we say the first two now and the rest at the Seder's conclusion). It's highly expressive and gives serious "propers," as Aretha Franklin sings in **"Respect,"** 𝄞 to the Almighty. If you want to recite part or all of it, the words are below. If not, feel free to sing along with the Queen.

LIFT UP YOUR SECOND CUP OF WINE:

Psalm 113

לְפִיכָךְ אֲנַחְנוּ חַיָּבִים לְהוֹדוֹת, לְהַלֵּל, לְשַׁבֵּחַ, לְפָאֵר, לְרוֹמֵם, לְהַדֵּר, לְבָרֵךְ, לְעַלֵּה וּלְקַלֵּס לְמִי שֶׁעָשָׂה לַאֲבוֹתֵינוּ וְלָנוּ אֶת כָּל הַנִּסִּים הָאֵלּוּ: הוֹצִיאָנוּ מֵעַבְדוּת לְחֵרוּת, מִיָּגוֹן לְשִׂמְחָה, וּמֵאֵבֶל לְיוֹם טוֹב, וּמֵאֲפֵלָה לְאוֹר גָּדוֹל, וּמִשִּׁעְבּוּד לִגְאֻלָּה. וְנֹאמַר לְפָנָיו שִׁירָה חֲדָשָׁה: הַלְלוּיָהּ.

Le'fee'chach ah'nach'noo
cha'yaveem l'ho'dote, l'ha'layl,
l'sha'bayach, l'fa'ayr, l'ro'maym,
l'ha'dayr, l'varaych, l'aleh oo'l'kalays
l'mee she'asah la'avotaynoo
v'lanoo et kol ha'neeseem ha'ayloo.
Hotzee'anoo may'avdoot l'chayroot
mee'yagone l'simcha, oo'may'ayvel
l'yom yov, oo'may'afayla l'or gadol,
oo'mee'shee'bood li'ge'oola.
Ve'nomar lefanav sheerah chadasha.

Therefore we are obligated to thank, praise, laud, glorify, exalt, lavish, bless, raise high, and acclaim the One who made all these miracles for our ancestors and for us: God brought us out from slavery to freedom, from sorrow to joy, from mourning to festival, from darkness to great light, and from bondage to redemption. And we will say a new song before God, Halleluyah!

הַלְלוּיָהּ הַלְלוּ עַבְדֵי יְיָ, הַלְלוּ אֶת שֵׁם יְיָ.

יְהִי שֵׁם יְיָ מְבֹרָךְ מֵעַתָּה וְעַד עוֹלָם.

מִמִּזְרַח שֶׁמֶשׁ עַד מְבוֹאוֹ מְהֻלָּל שֵׁם יְיָ.

רָם עַל כָּל גּוֹיִם יְיָ, עַל הַשָּׁמַיִם כְּבוֹדוֹ.

מִי כַּיְיָ אֱלֹהֵינוּ הַמַּגְבִּיהִי לָשָׁבֶת, הַמַּשְׁפִּילִי לִרְאוֹת בַּשָּׁמַיִם וּבָאָרֶץ?

מְקִימִי מֵעָפָר דָּל, מֵאַשְׁפֹּת יָרִים אֶבְיוֹן, לְהוֹשִׁיבִי עִם נְדִיבִים, עִם נְדִיבֵי עַמּוֹ.

מוֹשִׁיבִי עֲקֶרֶת הַבַּיִת, אֵם הַבָּנִים שְׂמֵחָה. הַלְלוּיָהּ.

Ha'le'looyah hal'loo av'day Adonoi,
hale'loo et shaym Adonoi.

Ye'hee shaym Adonoi me'vo'rach;
may'a'tah v'ad olam.

Mee'miz'rach shemesh ad mevo'o,
me'hoo'lal shaym Adonoi.

Ram al kol go'yeem Adonoi, al
ha'sha'ma'yeem ke'vo'do.

Mi ka'donoi e'lohay'noo;
ha'mag'bee'hee la'sha'vet.

Ha'mash'pee'lee lir'ot
ba'sha'ma'yeem oo'va'aretz.

Me'kee'mee may'afar dal,
may'ash'pot ya'reem ev'yon.

Le'ho'sheevee im ne'dee'veem, im
ne'dee'vay amo.

Mo'shee'vee a'keret ha'bayeet aym
ha'baneem s'maycha ha'l'loo'yah.

Halleluyah! [Praise Yah!] Praise,
servants of Adonoi, praise the name
of Adonoi.

May the Name of Adonoi be blessed
from now and forever.

From the rising of the sun in the East
to its setting, the name of Adonoi is
praised.

Elevated above all nations is Adonoi;
God's honor is above the heavens.

Who is like Adonoi, our God, who sits
on high,

Who looks down upon the heavens
and the earth?

God lifts up the poor from the dust;
from the refuse piles, God raises the
destitute.

To seat them with the nobles, with
the nobles of God's people.

God settles a barren woman in a
home, the mother of children is
happy. Praise Yah!

Psalm 114

בְּצֵאת יִשְׂרָאֵל מִמִּצְרָיִם, בֵּית יַעֲקֹב מֵעַם לֹעֵז,
הָיְתָה יְהוּדָה לְקָדְשׁוֹ, יִשְׂרָאֵל מַמְשְׁלוֹתָיו.

הַיָּם רָאָה וַיָּנֹס, הַיַּרְדֵּן יִסֹּב לְאָחוֹר.

הֶהָרִים רָקְדוּ כְאֵילִים, גְּבָעוֹת כִּבְנֵי צֹאן.

מַה לְּךָ הַיָּם כִּי תָנוּס, הַיַּרְדֵּן – תִּסֹּב לְאָחוֹר,
הֶהָרִים – תִּרְקְדוּ כְאֵילִים, גְּבָעוֹת כִּבְנֵי צֹאן.

מִלִּפְנֵי אָדוֹן חוּלִי אָרֶץ, מִלִּפְנֵי אֱלוֹהַּ יַעֲקֹב.

הַהֹפְכִי הַצּוּר אֲגַם מָיִם, חַלָּמִישׁ לְמַעְיְנוֹ מָיִם.

B'tzayt Yisra'ayl mee'mitz'ra'yim,
bayt Ya'a'kov may'am lo'ayz.

Ha'ye'tah Ye'hoo'dah l'kod'show,
Yisra'ayl mam'she'lo'tav.

Ha'yam ra'ah va'ya'nos, ha'yar'dayn
yeesov le'achor.

He'ha'reem ra'ke'doo che'ayleem,
ge'va'ot kiv'nay tzon.

Mah lecha ha'yam kee tanoos,
ha'yar'dayn tee'sov le'achor.

He'ha'reem tir'ke'doo che'ayleem,
ge'va'ot kiv'nay tzon.

Mee'lif'enay a'don choo'lee aretz,
mee'lif'enay elo'hai Ya'a'kov.

Ha'ho'fechee ha'tzoor agam mayim,
cha'la'meesh le'mai'no ma'yeem.

The Psalm That Rocks the Best

Psalm 114 may be the most rock 'n' roll psalm of all time, with its lyrical flow, chiaroscuro tone, and imagery. Seriously, it could be a Led Zeppelin song.

In Israel's going out from Egypt, the house of Jacob from people of a strange tongue,

Judah became God's sanctified one; Israel, God's dominion.

The sea saw them and fled, the Jordan River turned backward,

The mountains danced like rams, the hills like lambs.

What is happening to you, O Sea, that you flee,

The Jordan that you turn backward;

The mountains that dance like rams, the hills like lambs.

From before a Master, tremble, O earth, from before the God of Jacob.

The One who turns the boulder into a pond of water, the flint into a spring of water.

LIFT THE SECOND CUP OF WINE AND SAY:

בָּרוּךְ אַתָּה יְיָ, אֱלֹהֵינוּ מֶלֶךְ הָעוֹלָם, אֲשֶׁר גְּאָלָנוּ
וְגָאַל אֶת אֲבוֹתֵינוּ מִמִּצְרַיִם, וְהִגִּיעָנוּ הַלַּיְלָה הַזֶּה
לֶאֱכָל בּוֹ מַצָּה וּמָרוֹר. כֵּן יְיָ אֱלֹהֵינוּ וֵאלֹהֵי אֲבוֹתֵינוּ
יַגִּיעֵנוּ לְמוֹעֲדִים וְלִרְגָלִים אֲחֵרִים הַבָּאִים לִקְרָאתֵנוּ
לְשָׁלוֹם, שְׂמֵחִים בְּבִנְיַן עִירֶךָ וְשָׂשִׂים בַּעֲבוֹדָתֶךָ.
וְנֹאכַל שָׁם מִן הַזְּבָחִים וּמִן הַפְּסָחִים אֲשֶׁר יַגִּיעַ
דָּמָם עַל קִיר מִזְבַּחֲךָ לְרָצוֹן, וְנוֹדֶה לְךָ שִׁיר חָדָשׁ
עַל גְּאֻלָּתֵנוּ וְעַל פְּדוּת נַפְשֵׁנוּ. בָּרוּךְ אַתָּה יְיָ, גָּאַל
יִשְׂרָאֵל.

Baruch atah Adonoi, Elohaynoo Melech ha'olam, asher g'alanoo v'ga'al et avotaynoo mee'mitzrayim, v'higee'anoo la'lai'lah hazeh le'echol bo matzah oo'maror. Kayn Adonoi Elohaynoo vay'lohay avotaynoo yagi'aynoo l'mo'adeem v'lirgalim achayreem haba'eem lik'rataynoo l'shalom, s'maycheem b'vinyan eer'cha v'saseem ba'avodatecha. V'nochal sham min hazvacheem u'min ha'psacheem asher yagia damam al keer miz'bachacha l'ratzon,

v'nodeh l'cha sheer chadash al g'ulataynoo v'al p'doot nafshaynoo. Baruch Atah Adonoi, ga'al Yisrael.

Blessed are You, Adonoi our God, Ruler of the Universe, who redeemed us and redeemed our ancestors from Egypt, and brought us to this night to eat matzah and maror. So, too, Adonoi our God, and God of our ancestors, bring us to other appointed times and pilgrimages that come to greet us for peace, rejoicing in the building of Your city and happy in Your worship. We will eat there of the offerings and from the Passover offerings, whose blood shall reach the wall of Your altar for favor, and we will thank You with a new song for our redemption and for the redemption of our lives. Blessed are you, Adonoi, who redeemed Israel.

We say this blessing and then drink while reclining to the left:

בָּרוּךְ אַתָּה יְיָ, אֱלֹהֵינוּ מֶלֶךְ הָעוֹלָם, בּוֹרֵא פְּרִי
הַגָּפֶן.

Baruch atah Adonoi, Elohaynoo
Melech Ha'Olam, boray p'ree
ha'gafen.

Blessed are You, Adonoi, our God, Ruler
of the Universe, who creates the fruit
of the vine.

DRINK UP THAT SECOND CUP!

Rachtza: רָחְצָה
Second Ritual Handwashing

Pour water over alternating hands three times. "The Water Song" for this second
handwashing is a bracha:

בָּרוּךְ אַתָּה יְיָ, אֱלֹהֵינוּ מֶלֶךְ הָעוֹלָם, אֲשֶׁר קִדְּשָׁנוּ
בְּמִצְוֹתָיו וְצִוָּנוּ עַל נְטִילַת יָדָיִם.

Baruch ata Adonoi, Elohaynoo
melech ha'olam, asher kid'shanoo
b'mitzvotav v'tzeevanoo al n'teelat
yadai'yim.

Blessed are You, Adonoi our God,
Ruler of the Universe, who sanctified
us with His commandments and
commanded us on the washing of
hands.

SHHH! NO TALKING NOW. EVERYONE AT THE
TABLE IS SUPPOSED TO ACT LIKE THE
GO-GO'S IN **"OUR LIPS ARE SEALED,"** UNTIL
THE BLESSING OVER THE MATZAH IS SAID.

Motzi Matzah: מוֹצִיא מַצָּה

This is a double bracha: Hamotzi, which is the general blessing for bread, and a Pesach-specific blessing for the matzah. It may be read in unison, or the host may read it.

בָּרוּךְ אַתָּה יְיָ, אֱלֹהֵינוּ מֶלֶךְ הָעוֹלָם, הַמּוֹצִיא לֶחֶם מִן הָאָרֶץ.

Baruch ata Adonoi, Elohaynoo melech ha'olam, hamotzee lechem min ha'aretz.

Blessed are You, Adonoi our God, Ruler of the Universe, who brings forth bread from the earth.

בָּרוּךְ אַתָּה יְיָ, אֱלֹהֵינוּ מֶלֶךְ הָעוֹלָם, אֲשֶׁר קִדְּשָׁנוּ בְּמִצְוֹתָיו וְצִוָּנוּ עַל אֲכִילַת מַצָּה.

Baruch ata Adonoi, Elohaynoo melech ha'olam, asher kid'shanoo b'mitzvotav v'tzeevanoo al acheelat matzah.

Blessed are You, Adonoi our God, Ruler of the Universe, who sanctified us with His commandments and has commanded us on the eating of matzah.

YOU MAY NOW MUNCH YOUR MATZAH!

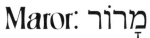

Maror: מָרוֹר
What Is It Good For?

The Jews in Egypt were in a Jam. Enslavement under Pharaoh was **"The Bitterest Pill."** 🎼

We eat maror, the bitter herb, to remember the suffering we went through, and we don't lean to the left this time. We do **"Da' Dip"** again, dipping an olive-sized piece of raw horseradish into the charoset to take the **"Bitter with the Sweet,"** like Carole King sings. An ounce of grated horseradish (the pickled, jarred stuff) is okay too, or a very large leaf of romaine lettuce if you really can't take the heat. Recite the following (either together, or the host may read and everyone else says "Amen"), then eat:

בָּרוּךְ אַתָּה יְיָ, אֱלֹהֵינוּ מֶלֶךְ הָעוֹלָם, אֲשֶׁר קִדְּשָׁנוּ בְּמִצְוֹתָיו וְצִוָּנוּ עַל אֲכִילַת מָרוֹר.

Baruch ata Adonoi, Elohaynoo melech haolam, ashayr kid'shanoo b'mitzvotav v'tzee'vanoo al a'chee'lat maror.

Blessed are You, Adonoi our God, Ruler of the Universe, who sanctified us with His commandments and commanded us on the eating of maror.

Korech: כּוֹרֵךְ Enjoy Every Hillel Sandwich

One of the most significant scholars in Jewish history, Hillel the Elder, is credited with inventing the shawarma, sandwiches, and a lot of very smart, empathetic sayings. He even had his own golden rule: "That which is hateful unto you, do not do to your neighbor. This is the whole of the Torah; the rest is commentary. Go forth and study."

Hillel's influence extends beyond Judaism and into the broader culture—literature, political thought, social life, even rock 'n' roll.

Named after the great sage, Hillel "Hilly" Kristal changed music forever when he opened the landmark New York club CBGB in 1973. He turned a scuzzy neighborhood biker bar into a launchpad for creative iconoclasts who blended pop, punk, poetry, philosophy, and art. There were many Jewish musicians in the bands Kristal helped propel to fame, including Blondie, the New York Dolls, the Ramones, and the Patti Smith Group.

The late Israeli American Red Hot Chili Peppers founder Hillel Slovak shared his name. He taught Flea to play bass and fed singer Anthony Kiedis. "Hillel was Jewish,"

Matzahchella, or Why Is This Fest Different from All Other Fests?

I s it the dusty desert of Indio, California, that makes the Coachella Valley Music and Arts Festival predisposed to a movable Pesach feast? Or is it the fact that the springtime event sometimes falls on the holiday?

The Coachella-Passover overlap left some Jewish festival attendees conflicted between rocking out to Guns N' Roses and partaking in a traditional Seder—until they figured out they were in the perfect place to celebrate: an expanse of desert populated by hungry amblers in various states of delirium.

In tonier areas of the polo club fairgrounds where Coachella is held, families may fork over hundreds of dollars for a chef-curated Seder within sprinting distance of the Mojave Tent. Farther out from the main events, anyone may attend a more succinct, populist ritual known as Matzahchella. Rami Matan Even-Esh, aka rapper Kosha Dillz, puts **"Big Matzah"** energy into creating the annual happening. Dressed like Moses, complete with a wig of flowing hair, beard, and a robe, Even-Esh has been hosting free mini-Seders at Coachella since 2016. He holds them at the Shabbat Tent, an itinerant lounge that sets up at cultural festivals throughout the year. Offering attendees Jewish prayers, kosher food, and a respite from the revelry, the tent began at the 1999 Phish millennium shows and now has a national presence.

Even-Esh has mastered the art of the ten-minute Seder (including gefilte fish, hard-boiled eggs, and other customary foods), which he repeats throughout the designated days. But his greatest innovation, perhaps, is transforming the Haggadah's prayer for Jews in the Diaspora into an invocation on behalf of concertgoers everywhere: "This year we are GA (General Admission)," he says. "And next year may we be VIP."

In the Book of Exodus, Moses and Aaron relay this message to Pharaoh from God: "Let my people go, so that they can celebrate a festival in the desert to honor me." Even Hallel mentions a festival. One might ask: Did the Almighty envision Coachella? Rock 'n' roll sages will ponder this now and in the future.

Kiedis says. "He looked Jewish, and talked about Jewish stuff, and the food in that kitchen was Jewish. He made us egg salad sandwiches on rye bread that day, which was totally exotic food to me then."

Calabasas, California, rock band Incubus named their seventh studio album *If Not Now, When?* after a novel by author/scientist/Holocaust survivor Primo Levi, who lifted his title from Hillel.

Hillel is buried in northern Israel; anyone can visit his sepulchre. His wise words, however, have been circulating since the time he said them, approximately 110 BCE–10 CE. And so has his fabled sandwich, which was most likely a shawarma to begin with.

During Pesach, Hillel either put a hunk of the sacrificed paschal lamb, when that was a thing, and bitter herb between two pieces of matzah, or he decided to **"Wrap It Up"** in a soft, flexible matzah. Whichever one he actually did, we honor him by re-creating his odd concoction, mixing foods that are symbolic of both freedom and enslavement.

Use the bottom matzah from your stack of three, and break it up so everyone gets two pieces. Put a piece of maror, dipped in charoset, in between, then lean, because Hillel leaned, and say this before you eat it:

This is what Hillel did, during the time the
temple stood. He wrapped paschal lamb, bitter herbs, and
matzah, and ate them together.

Warren Zevon, whose Jewish immigrant dad changed the family name from Zivotofsky, was also known to issue memorable maxims, like his song **"I'll Sleep When I'm Dead."** While making a TV appearance with David Letterman, who asked him about a recent terminal cancer diagnosis, he offered this piece of wisdom: "Enjoy every sandwich." It sounds very Hillel.

Why Wilco's Jeff Tweedy Converted to Judaism

A founding member of two influential Americana bands, Uncle Tupelo and Wilco, Belleville, Illinois-born Jeff Tweedy fell in love with and married Sue Miller, talent booker of the late, legendary Lounge Ax club in Chicago. He was moved by her strong Jewish identity and agreed to raise their children in the Jewish faith. When their younger son Sammy was working through his bar mitzvah preparation, Tweedy joined him at the Reform Congregation Emanuel on Chicago's North Side and began studying Judaism in earnest. Inspired by the theology of their synagogue's Rabbi Emeritus Herman Schaalman, Tweedy converted to Judaism in 2013.

Wilco continues to play and tour, but now music making is a family endeavor for Tweedy. He and Miller accomplished what many child-rearing guitarists hope for—they had a drummer. Son Spencer collaborates with his dad in the duo

Tweedy and drummed on Mavis Staples's *One True Vine*, which his dad played on and produced. Spencer and Sammy have their own duo as well. Do families who play together also "pray" together? According to Spencer, the Tweedys' Seder lore continues to expand with stories like this one:

My great uncle Paul is known for serving himself heroic portions of the traditional bitter herb —in our family, horseradish—not out of machismo but out of enthusiasm and perhaps a taste for the vegetable. One memorable year, Paul outdid himself with a hockey puck–sized disc of horseradish, eaten in one bite. He turned red, began coughing, doubled over, and couldn't speak. We nearly called nine-one-one. Luckily, Paul survived with a much-refreshed sinus system; we survived with a new traumatic memory to add to the pile.

The Shulchan Orech: שֻׁלְחָן עוֹרֵךְ

The Festive Meal

Its literal translation is "set table," but this is the point in the evening when most Haggadahs take a rest while everyone enjoys the festive meal. Since we're incorporating some new customs, though, we have stories to serve as aperitif and digestif, if you're so inclined.

Rapper/singer Drake has posted photos of his family Seders on social media, and he was "re-bar mitzvahed" in a 2011 music video.

The Duality of Blondshell

R aised in New York, based in Los Angeles, Sabrina Teitelbaum used to make pop music under the name BAUM. But her eponymous debut as Blondshell draws from guitar-driven '90s rock and the women who made it cool, like PJ Harvey and Courtney Love. It was released in April 2023 on Passover, which has particular meaning for Teitelbaum:

Passover sticks out in my mind as one of the more iconic Jewish holidays, particularly as someone who has loved to drink and recline. In my house it was a time when we got together with a big group of friends and family and enjoyed ourselves, but also got serious about the history. At the core of the holiday, it's a time to talk about the miracle of our existence in the face of so much persecution. That duality was a big part of the Judaism I grew up with—a celebration of our community and culture, a time to laugh, but also a time dedicated to making sure we knew our own past.

Rami Jaffee and the Magic of Jewish Soul Food

Rami Jaffee has played in two of the biggest rock bands of the last three decades: Foo Fighters and the Wallflowers. Between them both, he has taken home five Grammys. He has recorded with a galaxy of stars, from Johnny Cash to Neil Diamond to Selena Gomez. He is in the Rock & Roll Hall of Fame, inducted as a Foo Fighter by rock legend Paul McCartney. But even before these accolades, Jaffee managed to do what no other rock 'n' roller ever has—he got a Passover kugel into *Rolling Stone*.

The Wallflowers' star was rising, and the music magazine sent a reporter to follow them around on tour. The scribe took notice of the slab of Jewish soul food, a casserole of potatoes or noodles and eggs that may be sweet or savory. "It was my aunt Elaine's kugel," Jaffee says. "She delivered it to the bus during Passover."

If kugel magic is part of becoming a rock star, then bring it on. Jaffee's Judaism is as baked into him as his talent for playing any keyboard in existence. It makes him the guy in the band who adds not only shimmering textures to the music but also perspective and humor to the other twenty-three hours in the day. In the Foo Fighters' 2022 comedy/horror film *Studio 666*, which Jaffee says is "loosely based on our personalities," it emerges hilariously. "There's a scene where [Foo guitarist] Chris [Shiflett] says something dirty about my grandma," he says. "I rewrote the 'Stay away from my grandma' line to 'Stay away from my bubbe!'" And he delivered it with conviction. Jewish grandmas everywhere kvelled.

Jaffee's Ashkenazi roots, on his dad's side, are Ukraine via New York City (his mom is French/Moroccan). "My grandpa moved right into the Lower East Side in the early 1900s after escaping the hills of Kyiv," he says. Grandpa Jaffee's name was altered somewhere between boarding the ship that took him across the Atlantic Ocean and Ellis Island, but after such a lengthy journey he wasn't about to accept it. "He had no problem adding the *e* they took off," Jaffee says.

The future rocker grew up in Fairfax Village, a funky but chic parcel of Los Angeles between West Hollywood and La Brea, home to many Jewish families and the landmark ninety-plus-year-old, fourth-generation-run Canter's Deli. Renowned for pastrami and corned beef on rye and matzah ball soup, Canter's added on the Kibitz Room, a small cocktail lounge adjacent to its twenty-four-hour food service, in 1961. By the end of that decade, artists such as Janis Joplin, the Byrds, and the Doors were popping in post-gig for a bite and a drink.

FOOGEL·ICIOUS

kugel

One hundred people showed up to play at Rami Jaffee's first official jam at Canter's, including Lenny Kravitz and Red Hot Chili Peppers singer Anthony Kiedis.

It was the Kibitz Room where Jaffee met Jakob Dylan (son of music icon Bob), a singer/songwriter with a lightly reticent demeanor and salient blue eyes. They'd been teenagers who gravitated toward the bar's $1.30 beers, but that was the least of what they had in common. They were two Jewish sons of Los Angeles, born the same year: 1969. They were both in love with rootsy rock at the very moment that hair metal was in decline and grunge (including Jaffee's future bandmate, Foo Fighters founder/ Nirvana drummer Dave Grohl) was ascending. In other words, record labels weren't exactly looking for the Wallflowers in 1990. Such is a conundrum of Gen X; born during a baby bust, its members sometimes land in the right place at the wrong time.

But they were also both ambitious. A Canter's waiter played jazz in the Kibitz Room every Monday night. Jaffee asked Marc Canter, his old friend from Little League baseball and Fairfax High School, if he could have a Tuesday night for his "twenty-first birthday party jam," he says, which turned into a weekly jam, which became a happening. "[After] starting an incredible music scene all from the back of Canter's Deli, how does one not feel Jewish?" he says.

The Wallflowers eventually found their time with their second album, *Bringing Down the Horse* (1996), which sold nearly five million copies. Not long after, radio personality Howard Stern heard Jaffee was trekking through Nepal and jokingly called him the "Rami Lama" without realizing how well the nickname fit Jaffee's innate spirituality.

"I was bar mitzvahed, but I've seen many a Jew disappear from being Jewish the day after their bar mitzvah," he says. "I just seemed to soak in it in a special way to this day."

The Supermensch, the Rock Star, and the Chicken

Show business legend Shep Gordon was in New York City, searching for Passover sustenance, in the spring of 2014. He was in town for the screening of his biopic, *Supermensch: The Legend of Shep Gordon* (directed by actor/comic Mike Myers and Beth Aala) at the Tribeca Film Festival, which overlapped with the holiday. Gordon, while spiritually known as a JewBu (Jewish Buddhist) according to his movie star friend Michael Douglas, is also known to observe Jewish holidays in some way, wherever he may be. One Yom Kippur, the holiest day of the year for Jews, he accompanied City Winery's Michael Dorf and family to Lab/Shul, a New York–based, artist-driven, highly inclusive pop-up "house" of worship, where holding hands was part of the service.

Gordon grew up in New York; it's still audible in his voice. He moved to Hollywood in the late 1960s, partied with Jimi Hendrix and Janis Joplin, and went into the entertainment management business, handling everyone from Luther Vandross to his most notorious rock 'n' roll client, Alice Cooper, aka Vincent Furnier. Cooper was propelled to shock rock infamy by his theatrical presentation and an urban legend involving a chicken that Gordon had tossed onstage.

Cooper's documentary, *Super Duper Alice Cooper*, was also being screened at the film fest that year. He joined Gordon, who is still his manager and a lifelong friend, at Kutsher's Tribeca for chopped chicken liver on matzah.

Led by his interest in fine food, Gordon pivoted his career in the 1980s to hyping chefs. He made rock stars of Wolfgang Puck, Emeril Lagasse, and others, helping to transform the culinary industry into the celebrity culture it is today. In 2020, his foodie love was on display when he Zoomed into the City Winery Virtual Seder from the verdant lawn of his home in Maui. On a table in front of him was a giant bowl of chicken soup. Talking about his grandmother's recipe, he made it clear that this generational cure-all is effective for treating not only physical ailments but also spiritual ones.

Tzafun: צָפוּן

Finding and Eating the Afikomen

The eating portion of the Seder wraps with a bite of matzah and a bit of **"Hide and Seek."** It's traditionally a time for the kids at the table to look for the half piece of matzah that was hidden earlier in the night, but anyone can participate.

DISPATCH THE AFIKOMEN
SEEKERS NOW!

As ABBA says, **"The Winner Takes It All"**; a cash reward is usually exchanged for the afikomen. After it's found, break it up into "Bits and Pieces" for everyone to share. There is historical disparity over the timing of the afikomen, with some scholars claiming it must not be eaten "After Midnight," and others saying it's fine to have it **"All Night Long."** ♪ Go with whichever song you favor.

Barech: בָּרֵךְ
Birkat Hamazon

Jews say grace *after* meals. It's not because we can't wait to eat, as we just proved with an extended pining for dinner at our Seder, not to mention all the blessings we recite that put a delay on consuming wine, bread, and other things. Eating before saying grace is written in Deuteronomy, the fifth book of the Torah:

> *When you have eaten and are satisfied, you shall bless*
> *the Lord your God for the good land which He gave you.*

Birkat Hamazon, which gives thanks not only for the food but also for the land of Israel, is said after any meal containing bread, leavened or not, but it has particular relevance to Passover. Deuteronomy marks the end of the Jews' forty-year desert odyssey and their entrance into the Promised Land, and this thanks-giving instruction comes from Moses. Already aware that he will not be allowed to enter, Moses passes along all the rules and regulations given to him by God on how the Jewish people are to comport themselves, covering everything from civil and criminal law to kashruth and other religious observances. He hands the mantle of power to Joshua (yes, the one who "fought the battle of Jericho") and then dies, and it is said that he is buried by God Himself.

On Shabbat and certain Jewish holidays, Birkat Hamazon is preceded by Psalm 126 ("Shir Hamaalot") from "A Song of Ascents," fifteen psalms that are thought to have been sung by Jews on their way up to the Holy Temple during the three annual festival holidays, including Pesach, though there are many other exegeses. We love the Talmud story about Honi HaMe'agel, a first-century BCE scholar who was kind of obsessed with the first line of Psalm 126: "When Adonoi brings the return to Zion, we will be like dreamers."

Honi wondered if it was possible for life to be like a dream. In one version of the tale, he eats a meal and then falls asleep for seventy years—which is exactly how you may feel right now, having just partaken in the shulchan orech. In this parable, Honi talks with a man planting a little carob tree, only to find the man's grandson harvesting its fruit seventy years later. Likewise, we make a considerable effort in preparing for and performing the rituals of Passover to retell the Exodus story, so that future generations may glean insight into what it means to be part of this tribe.

Psalm 126

שִׁיר הַמַּעֲלוֹת, בְּשׁוּב יְיָ אֶת שִׁיבַת צִיּוֹן הָיִינוּ כְּחֹלְמִים.

אָז יִמָּלֵא שְׂחוֹק פִּינוּ וּלְשׁוֹנֵנוּ רִנָּה.

אָז יֹאמְרוּ בַגּוֹיִם: הִגְדִּיל יְיָ לַעֲשׂוֹת עִם אֵלֶּה.

הִגְדִּיל יְיָ לַעֲשׂוֹת עִמָּנוּ, הָיִינוּ שְׂמֵחִים.

שׁוּבָה יְיָ אֶת שְׁבִיתֵנוּ כַּאֲפִיקִים בַּנֶּגֶב.

הַזֹּרְעִים בְּדִמְעָה, בְּרִנָּה יִקְצֹרוּ.

הָלוֹךְ יֵלֵךְ וּבָכֹה נֹשֵׂא מֶשֶׁךְ הַזָּרַע, בֹּא יָבֹא בְרִנָּה נֹשֵׂא אֲלֻמֹּתָיו.

Sheer ha'ma'alot b'shoov Adonoi et sheevat tzee'yon hayeenoo ke'chol'meem.

Az yimalay schok feenu ul'shonaynoo reena az yom'roo va'goyeem

Higdeel Adonoi la'asot im ayleh.

Higdeel Adonoi la'asot eemanoo ha'yeenoo semaycheem.

Shoovah Adonoi et sheveetaynoo ka'afeekeem ba'negev.

Ha'zoreem be'dimah be'reena yik'tzo'roo.

Ha'low'ch yaylaych oo'va'cho nosay meshech ha'zara bo yavo ve'reenah nosay a'loomo'tav.

A Song of Ascents; When Adonoi brings the return to Zion, we will be like dreamers.

Then our mouths will be full of joy and our tongues joyful melody;

Then they will say among the nations, "Adonoi has done greatly with these."

Adonoi has done greatly with us; we are happy.

Adonoi, return our captivity like streams in the desert.

Those that sow with weeping will reap with joyful song.

The one who goes and cries, he carries the measure of seed,

Will surely come in joyful song, carrying his sheaves.

The Birkat Hamazon itself is sung in four parts, a lengthy benediction that R&B greats Sam and Dave would've wrapped up by simply saying **"I Thank You."**

Here's part one, which starts with a little call-and-response and is then sung or recited together (the rest may be read together, or to oneself while enjoying **"The Sound of Silence"**).

The leader says:

רַבּוֹתַי נְבָרֵךְ

Rabbotai nevaraych

My masters, let's bless:

All those present answer:

יְהִי שֵׁם יְיָ מְבֹרָךְ מֵעַתָּה וְעַד עוֹלָם.

Yehee shaym Adonoi mevorach may'ata v'ad olam.

May the name of Adonoi be blessed now and forever [Psalm 113:2].

The host says:

בִּרְשׁוּת מָרָנָן וְרַבָּנָן וְרַבּוֹתַי, נְבָרֵךְ [אֱלֹהֵינוּ] שֶׁאָכַלְנוּ מִשֶּׁלּוֹ.

Bir'shoot maranan v'rabanan v'rabotai, nevarach [Elohaynoo] she'achalnoo mee'shelo.

With the permission of our masters and our teachers and my rabbis, let us bless [our God] from whom we have eaten.

Those present answer:

בָּרוּךְ [אֱלֹהֵינוּ] שֶׁאָכַלְנוּ מִשֶּׁלּוֹ וּבְטוּבוֹ חָיִינוּ.

Baruch [Elohaynoo] she'achalnoo mee'shelo oov'too'vo chayeenoo.

Blessed is [our God] of whose we have eaten and by whose goodness we have lived.

The leader repeats:

בָּרוּךְ [אֱלֹהֵינוּ] שֶׁאָכַלְנוּ מִשֶּׁלּוֹ וּבְטוּבוֹ חָיִינוּ.

Baruch [Elohaynoo] she'achalnoo mee'shelo oov'too'vo chayeenoo.

Blessed is [our God] of whose we have eaten and by whose goodness we have lived.

All say:

בָּרוּךְ אַתָּה יְיָ, אֱלֹהֵינוּ מֶלֶךְ הָעוֹלָם, הַזָּן אֶת הָעוֹלָם כֻּלּוֹ בְּטוּבוֹ בְּחֵן בְּחֶסֶד וּבְרַחֲמִים, הוּא נוֹתֵן לֶחֶם לְכָל בָּשָׂר כִּי לְעוֹלָם חַסְדּוֹ. וּבְטוּבוֹ הַגָּדוֹל תָּמִיד לֹא חָסַר לָנוּ, וְאַל יֶחְסַר לָנוּ מָזוֹן לְעוֹלָם וָעֶד. בַּעֲבוּר שְׁמוֹ הַגָּדוֹל, כִּי הוּא אֵל זָן וּמְפַרְנֵס לַכֹּל וּמֵטִיב לַכֹּל, וּמֵכִין מָזוֹן לְכָל בְּרִיּוֹתָיו אֲשֶׁר בָּרָא. בָּרוּךְ אַתָּה יְיָ, הַזָּן אֶת הַכֹּל.

Baruch atah Adonoi, Elohaynoo melech ha'olam, hazan et ha'olam koolo b'toovo,

b'chayn b'chesed oov'rachameem.

Hoo notayn lechem l'chol basar, kee l'olam chasdo,

Oov'too'vo hagadol tameed lo chasar lanoo

v'al yechsar lanoo mazon l'olam va'ed.

Ba'avoor sh'mo hagadol, kee hoo Ayl zan oom'farnays lakol,

Oo'mayteev lakol oo'maycheen mazon l'chol b'reeyotav asher bara.

Baruch atah Adonoi, hazan et hakol.

Blessed are You, Adonoi our God, Ruler of the Universe, who nourishes the world entirely with His goodness, with grace, with lovingkindness, and with mercy; God gives bread to all flesh, for God's lovingkindness is eternal. And in God's great goodness, we have never lacked, and may we not lack food forever and ever. Because of God's great name, for God is a God that nourishes and provides support for all and does good for all and prepares food for all of God's creatures that God created. Blessed are You, Adonoi, who nourishes all.

Parts two, three, and four:

נוֹדֶה לְּךָ יְיָ אֱלֹהֵינוּ עַל שֶׁהִנְחַלְתָּ לַאֲבוֹתֵינוּ אֶרֶץ חֶמְדָּה טוֹבָה וּרְחָבָה, וְעַל שֶׁהוֹצֵאתָנוּ יְיָ אֱלֹהֵינוּ מֵאֶרֶץ מִצְרַיִם, וּפְדִיתָנוּ מִבֵּית עֲבָדִים, וְעַל בְּרִיתְךָ שֶׁחָתַמְתָּ בִּבְשָׂרֵנוּ, וְעַל תּוֹרָתְךָ שֶׁלִּמַּדְתָּנוּ, וְעַל חֻקֶּיךָ שֶׁהוֹדַעְתָּנוּ, וְעַל חַיִּים חֵן וָחֶסֶד שֶׁחוֹנַנְתָּנוּ, וְעַל אֲכִילַת מָזוֹן שָׁאַתָּה זָן וּמְפַרְנֵס אוֹתָנוּ תָּמִיד, בְּכָל יוֹם וּבְכָל עֵת וּבְכָל שָׁעָה:

Nodeh l'cha, Adonoi elo'haynoo, al she'hin'chalta la'avotaynoo eretz chemda tovah oo'rechava, v'al she'hotzaytanoo Adonoi Elohaynoo may'eretz mitz'rayeem, uf'deetanoo meebayt avadeem, v'al breet'cha she'chatamta biv'saraynoo, v'al torat'cha she'leemad'tanoo, v'al chookecha she'hodatanoo, v'al chayim chayn va'chesed she'chonantanoo, v'al acheelat mazon she'atah zan, oo'mefarnays otanoo tameed, b'chol yom, oo'v'chol ayt oo'v'chol sha'ah.

We will thank you, Adonoi our God, that you have bequeathed to our ancestors a lovely, good, and spacious land, and that You took us out, Adonoi our God, from the land of Egypt and that You redeemed us from the house of bondage, and for Your covenant which You signed in our flesh, and for Your Torah that You taught us, and for Your statutes which You made known to us, and for

life, grace, and lovingkindness with which You have endowed us, and for the eating of food that You feed and provide for us always, on every day, and at every time and in every hour.

וְעַל הַכֹּל יְיָ אֱלֹהֵינוּ, אֲנַחְנוּ מוֹדִים לָךְ וּמְבָרְכִים אוֹתָךְ, יִתְבָּרַךְ שִׁמְךָ בְּפִי כָּל חַי תָּמִיד לְעוֹלָם וָעֶד. כַּכָּתוּב: וְאָכַלְתָּ וְשָׂבָעְתָּ וּבֵרַכְתָּ אֶת יְיָ אֱלֹהֶיךָ עַל הָאָרֶץ הַטֹּבָה אֲשֶׁר נָתַן לָךְ. בָּרוּךְ אַתָּה יְיָ, עַל הָאָרֶץ וְעַל הַמָּזוֹן:

V'al hakol, Adonoi Elo'haynoo, anachnoo modeem lach, oo'mevarcheem otach, yit'barach shim'cha b'fee kol chai tameed l'olam va'ed, kakatoov v'achalata, v'savata, oovayrachta et Adonoi Elohecha al ha'aretz ha'tovah asher natan lach, baruch atah, Adonoi, al ha'aretz v'al hamazon.

And for everything, Adonoi our God, we thank You and bless You; may Your name be blessed by the mouth of all that lives, always and eternally, as it is written [Deuteronomy 8:10]: "And you shall eat and you shall be satisfied and you shall bless Adonoi your God for the good land that He gave you." Blessed are You, Adonoi, for the land and for the nourishment.

רַחֵם נָא יְיָ אֱלֹהֵינוּ עַל יִשְׂרָאֵל עַמֶּךָ וְעַל יְרוּשָׁלַיִם עִירֶךָ וְעַל צִיּוֹן מִשְׁכַּן כְּבוֹדֶךָ וְעַל מַלְכוּת בֵּית דָּוִד מְשִׁיחֶךָ וְעַל הַבַּיִת הַגָּדוֹל וְהַקָּדוֹשׁ שֶׁנִּקְרָא שִׁמְךָ עָלָיו: אֱלֹהֵינוּ אָבִינוּ, רְעֵנוּ זוּנֵנוּ פַּרְנְסֵנוּ וְכַלְכְּלֵנוּ וְהַרְוִיחֵנוּ, וְהַרְוַח לָנוּ יְיָ אֱלֹהֵינוּ מְהֵרָה מִכָּל צָרוֹתֵינוּ. וְנָא אַל תַּצְרִיכֵנוּ יְיָ אֱלֹהֵינוּ, לֹא לִידֵי מַתְּנַת בָּשָׂר וָדָם וְלֹא לִידֵי הַלְוָאָתָם, כִּי אִם לְיָדְךָ הַמְּלֵאָה הַפְּתוּחָה הַקְּדוֹשָׁה וְהָרְחָבָה, שֶׁלֹּא נֵבוֹשׁ וְלֹא נִכָּלֵם לְעוֹלָם וָעֶד.

Rachaym na Adonoi Elohaynoo al Yisra'ayl amecha, ve'al Yerooshalayim ee'recha, v'al tzeeyon mishkan

kevodecha, va'al malchoot bayt
Daveed meshee'che'cha, v'al
habayeet hagadol ve'hakadosh
she'nikra shimcha alav. Elohaynu,
aveenu, re'aynoo, zoo'naynoo,
farnesaynoo vechal'kalaynoo
ve'harvee'chaynoo, ve'harvach lanoo
Adonoi Elohaynoo me'hayra meekol
tzarotaynoo. V'na al tazreechaynoo,
Adonoi Elohaynoo, lo leeday
matnat basar vadam velo leeday
halvatam, kee im l'yadcha, ha'melaya,
hapetoocha, hakedosha ve'harchava,
shelo nayvosh velo neekalaym le'olam
va'ed.

Please have compassion, Adonoi
our God, for Israel Your people, for
Jerusalem, Your city, and for Zion,
the dwelling place of Your Glory, and
for the sovereignty of the House
of David, Your anointed one; and
upon the great and holy house upon
which Your name is called. Our God,
our parent, shepherd us, nourish us,
provide for us, relieve us and relieve
us quickly, Adonoi, of all our troubles.
And please do not obligate us, Adonoi
our God, to gifts of flesh and blood,
or to their loans, but rather to Your
full, open, holy, and spacious hand, so
that we not be embarrassed and we
not be ashamed forever and ever.

On Shabbat, add:

רְצֵה וְהַחֲלִיצֵנוּ יְיָ אֱלֹהֵינוּ בְּמִצְוֹתֶיךָ וּבְמִצְוַת יוֹם
הַשְּׁבִיעִי הַשַּׁבָּת הַגָּדוֹל וְהַקָּדוֹשׁ הַזֶּה. כִּי יוֹם זֶה
גָּדוֹל וְקָדוֹשׁ הוּא לְפָנֶיךָ לִשְׁבָּת בּוֹ וְלָנוּחַ בּוֹ
בְּאַהֲבָה כְּמִצְוַת רְצוֹנֶךָ. וּבִרְצוֹנְךָ הָנִיחַ לָנוּ יְיָ
אֱלֹהֵינוּ שֶׁלֹּא תְהֵא צָרָה וְיָגוֹן וַאֲנָחָה בְּיוֹם
מְנוּחָתֵנוּ. וְהַרְאֵנוּ יְיָ אֱלֹהֵינוּ בְּנֶחָמַת צִיּוֹן עִירֶךָ
וּבְבִנְיַן יְרוּשָׁלַיִם עִיר קָדְשֶׁךָ כִּי אַתָּה הוּא בַּעַל
הַיְשׁוּעוֹת וּבַעַל הַנֶּחָמוֹת.

R'tzay v'ha'cha'tzeelaynoo
Adonoi Elohaynoo b'mitzvo'techa
oo'v'mitz'vat yom ha'sh'vee'ee,
hashabat hagadol v'hakadosh hazeh.
Kee yom zeh gadol v'kadosh hoo
l'fanecha, lish'bot bo v'lanoo'ach
bo b'ahavah k'mitzvat r'tzonecha.
Oo'virtzon'cha ha'nee'ach lanoo,
Adonoi Elohaynoo, she'lo t'hay
tzarah v'yagon v'anacha b'yom
m'noo'chataynoo. V'haraynoo Adonoi
Elohaynoo b'nechamat tzeeyon
eerecha, u'vevinyan Yerooshalayim
eer kod'shecha, kee atah hoo ba'al
ha'yishoo'ot oo'va'al hanechamot.

May You desire to strengthen
us, Adonoi our God, with your
commandments and with the
commandment of the seventh day, of
this great and holy Shabbat, for this
day is great and holy before You, to
cease work in it and to rest in it, with
love, according to the commandment
of Your will. And with Your will, allow
for us, Adonoi our God, that there
should not be trouble, grief, and
sighing on the day of our rest. And
may You show us, Adonoi our God,
the consolation of Zion, Your city,
and the rebuilding of Jerusalem, Your
holy city; since You are the Master
of salvations and the Master of
consolations.

אֱלֹהֵינוּ וֵאלֹהֵי אֲבוֹתֵינוּ, יַעֲלֶה וְיָבֹא וְיַגִּיעַ וְיֵרָאֶה
וְיֵרָצֶה וְיִשָּׁמַע וְיִפָּקֵד וְיִזָּכֵר זִכְרוֹנֵנוּ וּפִקְדוֹנֵנוּ, וְזִכְרוֹן
אֲבוֹתֵינוּ, וְזִכְרוֹן מָשִׁיחַ בֶּן דָּוִד עַבְדֶּךָ, וְזִכְרוֹן
יְרוּשָׁלַיִם עִיר קָדְשֶׁךָ, וְזִכְרוֹן כָּל עַמְּךָ בֵּית יִשְׂרָאֵל
לְפָנֶיךָ, לִפְלֵיטָה לְטוֹבָה לְחֵן וּלְחֶסֶד וּלְרַחֲמִים,
לְחַיִּים וּלְשָׁלוֹם בְּיוֹם חַג הַמַּצּוֹת הַזֶּה זָכְרֵנוּ יְיָ
אֱלֹהֵינוּ בּוֹ לְטוֹבָה וּפָקְדֵנוּ בוֹ לִבְרָכָה וְהוֹשִׁיעֵנוּ בוֹ
לְחַיִּים. וּבִדְבַר יְשׁוּעָה וְרַחֲמִים חוּס וְחָנֵּנוּ וְרַחֵם
עָלֵינוּ וְהוֹשִׁיעֵנוּ, כִּי אֵלֶיךָ עֵינֵינוּ, כִּי אֵל מֶלֶךְ חַנּוּן
וְרַחוּם אָתָּה. וּבְנֵה יְרוּשָׁלַיִם עִיר הַקֹּדֶשׁ בִּמְהֵרָה
בְיָמֵינוּ. בָּרוּךְ אַתָּה יְיָ, בּוֹנֵה בְרַחֲמָיו יְרוּשָׁלָיִם. אָמֵן.

Elohaynoo Vaylohay avotaynoo, ya'aleh v'yavo, v'yagee'a, v'yayra'eh, v'yay'ratzeh, v'yeeshama, v'yeepakayd, v'yeezachayr, zich'ronaynoo ufik'donanynoo, v'zich'ron avotaynoo, v'zich'ron mashee'ach ben David av'decha, v'zich'ron Yerushalayim eer kod'shecha, v'zich'ron kol am'cha bayt Yisrael l'fanecha, lif'laytah, l'tovah, l'chayn oo'l'chesed oo'l'rachamim, l'chayeem oo'l'shalom, b'yom chag hamatzot hazeh. Zoch'raynoo Adonai Elohaynoo bo l'tovah, oo'fok'daynoo vo liv'rachah, v'hoshee'aynoo vo l'chayeem, uvid'var yeshoo'ah v'rachameem, choos v'chonaynoo v'rachaym alaynoo v'hoshi'aynoo kee aylecha aynaynoo, ki Ayl Melech chanoon v'rachoom Atah. Oo'venay Yerushalayim eer hakodesh bimhayrah v'yamaynoo. Baruch atah Adonoi, boneh berachamav Yerushalyim. Amen.

Our God and God of our ancestors, may there ascend to you the remembrance of our ancestors; the remembrance of David, Your servant; the remembrance of Jerusalem, Your holy city; and the remembrance of Your entire people, the House of Israel, before You; for favor, life, and peace on this day of Rosh Chodesh/ the Festival of Pesach/the Festival of Sukkot. Remember us, Adonai our God, on this day for good; be mindful of us on this day for blessing; deliver us for life. As You promised salvation and mercy, be compassionate to us and deliver us. Our eyes are directed to You, because You are the Almighty Who Is King, gracious, and compassionate.

Our God and God of our ancestors, may there arise and come and reach and be seen and be acceptable and be heard and be counted, recalled and be remembered—our memory and pledge, and the memory of our ancestors, and the memory of the messiah, the son of David, Your servant; and the memory of Jerusalem, Your holy city; and the memory of all Your people, the house of Israel before You, for a remnant, for good, for grace, and for lovingkindness, and for mercy, for life, and for peace on this day of the Festival of Matzot. Remember us on it, Adonoi our God, for good and recall us on it for blessing and save us on it for life. And with a word of salvation and compassion, have mercy, favor us, and save us, for our eyes are to You, since You are a gracious and compassionate Ruler. And may You build Jerusalem, the holy city, speedily and in our days. Blessed are You, Adonoi, who builds Jerusalem with Your mercy. Amen.

בָּרוּךְ אַתָּה יְיָ, אֱלֹהֵינוּ מֶלֶךְ הָעוֹלָם, הָאֵל אָבִינוּ מַלְכֵּנוּ אַדִירֵנוּ בּוֹרְאֵנוּ גּוֹאֲלֵנוּ יוֹצְרֵנוּ קְדוֹשֵׁנוּ קְדוֹשׁ יַעֲקֹב רוֹעֵנוּ רוֹעֵה יִשְׂרָאֵל הַמֶּלֶךְ הַטּוֹב וְהַמֵּטִיב לַכֹּל שֶׁבְּכָל יוֹם וָיוֹם הוּא הֵטִיב, הוּא מֵטִיב, הוּא יֵיטִיב לָנוּ. הוּא גְמָלָנוּ הוּא גוֹמְלֵנוּ הוּא יִגְמְלֵנוּ לָעַד, לְחֵן וּלְחֶסֶד וּלְרַחֲמִים וּלְרֶוַח הַצָּלָה וְהַצְלָחָה, בְּרָכָה וִישׁוּעָה נֶחָמָה פַּרְנָסָה וְכַלְכָּלָה וְרַחֲמִים וְחַיִּים וְשָׁלוֹם וְכָל טוֹב, וּמִכָּל טוּב לְעוֹלָם עַל יְחַסְּרֵנוּ.

Baruch atah Adonoi, Elohaynoo melech ha'olam, ha'ayl aveenoo malkaynoo, adeeraynoo, boraynoo, go'alaynoo, yotzraynoo, kedoshaynoo kedosh Yaakov, ro'aynoo ro'ay Yisra'ayl, hamelech ha tov vehamayteev lakol, shebechol yom

vayom, hoo hayteev, hoo mayteev,
hoo yayteev lanoo, hoo g'malanoo,
hoo g'ma'laynoo, hoo yig'melaynoo
la'ad, l'chayn, oo'le'chesed
oo'le'rachameem, oo'le'revach
hatzalah ve'hatzlacha b'rachah
vee'shoo'ah, nechamah, parnasah,
ve'chalkalah, ve'rachameem,
ve'chayeem ve'shalom ve'chol
tov, oo'mee'kol toov le'olam al
yi'chasraynoo.

Blessed are You, Adonoi our God,
Ruler of the Universe, the God who
is our Parent, our Ruler, our Mighty
One, our Creator, our Redeemer,
our Maker, our Holy One, the Holy
One of Ya'akov, our Shepherd the
Shepherd of Israel, the good Ruler
who does good to all, since on each
and every day God has done good,
God does good, God will do good, for
us. God has requited us, God requites
us, God will requite us forever, for
grace and for lovingkindness, and
for mercy, and for relief, rescue,
and success, blessing and salvation,
consolation, livelihood and provision
and relief and compassion and life
and peace and all good; and forever
may we not lack any good.

הָרַחֲמָן הוּא יִמְלֹךְ עָלֵינוּ לְעוֹלָם וָעֶד.

Ha'rachaman hoo yimloch alaynoo
l'olam va'ed,

The Compassionate One will rule
over us forever.

הָרַחֲמָן הוּא יִתְבָּרֵךְ בַּשָּׁמַיִם וּבָאָרֶץ.

Ha'rachaman hoo yitbarach
ba'shama'yeem u'va'aretz.

May the Compassionate One be
blessed in the heavens and the earth.

הָרַחֲמָן הוּא יִשְׁתַּבַּח לְדוֹר דּוֹרִים, וְיִתְפָּאַר בָּנוּ
לָעַד וּלְנֵצַח נְצָחִים, וְיִתְהַדַּר בָּנוּ לָעַד וּלְעוֹלְמֵי
עוֹלָמִים.

Ha'rachaman hoo yishtabach
l'dor dorim, v'yitpa'ar banoo la'ad
oo'le'netzach n'tzacheem, v'yit'hadar
banoo la'ad oo'le'olmay olamim.

May the Compassionate One
be praised for generation upon
generation, and be exalted among us
forever and for all eternities, and be
glorified among us always and for all.

הָרַחֲמָן הוּא יְבָרֵךְ אֶת מְדִינַת יִשְׂרָאֵל וְאֶת אַחֵינוּ
וְאַחְיוֹתֵינוּ בְּרַחֲבֵי הָעוֹלָם.

Ha'rachaman hoo y'varaych et
medeenat Yisrael v'et achaynoo
v'achyotaynoo b'rochvei ha'olam.

הָרַחֲמָן הוּא יְפַרְנְסֵנוּ בְּכָבוֹד.

Ha'rachaman hoo y'far'nesaynoo
b'chavod.

May the Compassionate One sustain
us with honor.

הָרַחֲמָן הוּא יִשְׁבּוֹר עֻלֵּנוּ מֵעַל צַוָּארֵנוּ, וְהוּא
יוֹלִיכֵנוּ קוֹמְמִיּוּת לְאַרְצֵנוּ.

Ha'rachaman hoo yishbor oo'laynoo
may'al tza'va'raynoo, v'hoo
yolee'chaynoo ko'me'meeyoot
l'artzaynoo.

May the Compassionate One break
our yoke from upon our necks and
lead us upright to our land.

הָרַחֲמָן הוּא יִשְׁלַח לָנוּ בְּרָכָה מְרֻבָּה בַּבַּיִת הַזֶּה,
וְעַל שֻׁלְחָן זֶה שֶׁאָכַלְנוּ עָלָיו.

Ha'rachaman hoo yishlach b'rachah
m'roobah babayit hazeh, v'al
shoolchan zeh she'achalnoo alav.

124

May the Compassionate One send for us multiplied blessings in this home and upon this table upon which we have eaten.

הָרַחֲמָן הוּא יִשְׁלַח לָנוּ אֶת אֵלִיָּהוּ הַנָּבִיא זָכוּר לַטּוֹב, וִיבַשֶּׂר לָנוּ בְּשׂוֹרוֹת טוֹבוֹת יְשׁוּעוֹת וְנֶחָמוֹת.

Ha'rachaman hoo yishlach lanoo et Eliyahoo HaNavi, zachoor latov, vee'vaser lanoo b'sorot tovot, y'shoo'ot v'nechamot.

May the Compassionate One send us Eliyahu the prophet, remembered for the good, and he will announce to us good tidings of salvation and of consolation.

הָרַחֲמָן הוּא יְבָרֵךְ אֶת בַּעֲלִי / אִשְׁתִּי.

Ha'rachaman hoo yivaraych et ba'alee/eeshtee.

May the Compassionate One bless my husband/my wife.

הָרַחֲמָן הוּא יְבָרֵךְ אֶת [אָבִי מוֹרִי] בַּעַל הַבַּיִת הַזֶּה, וְאֶת [אִמִּי מוֹרָתִי] בַּעֲלַת הַבַּיִת הַזֶּה, אוֹתָם וְאֶת בֵּיתָם וְאֶת זַרְעָם וְאֶת כָּל אֲשֶׁר לָהֶם.

Ha'rachaman hoo yivaraych et [avee moree] ba'al habayit hazeh, ve'et [eemee moratee] ba'alat habayit hazeh, otam v'et baytam v'et zar'am v'et kol asher lahem.

May the Compassionate One bless [my father, my teacher,] the master of this home and [my mother, my teacher,] the mistress of this home, them and their household and their offspring and everything that is theirs.

אוֹתָנוּ וְאֶת כָּל אֲשֶׁר לָנוּ, כְּמוֹ שֶׁנִּתְבָּרְכוּ אֲבוֹתֵינוּ אַבְרָהָם יִצְחָק וְיַעֲקֹב, וְאִמּוֹתֵינוּ שָׂרָה רִבְקָה רָחֵל וְלֵאָה, בַּכֹּל מִכֹּל כֹּל, כֵּן יְבָרֵךְ אוֹתָנוּ כֻּלָּנוּ יַחַד בִּבְרָכָה שְׁלֵמָה, וְנֹאמַר, אָמֵן.

Otanoo v'et kol asher lanoo, k'mo she'nit'bar'choo avotaynoo Avraham, Yitzchak, v'Yaakov, v'eemotaynoo Sarah, Rivkah, Rachayl v'Lay'ah, bakol mee'kol kol, kayn y'va'raych o'tanoo koolanoo yachad, bi'vrachah sh'laymah, v'nomar: Amen.

Us and all that we have, as our fathers Avraham, Yitzchak, and Ya'akov, and our mothers Sarah, Rivka, Rachel, and Leah, were blessed with everything, from all of everything, so too may God bless us, all of us together, with a complete blessing and we shall say, Amen.

בַּמָּרוֹם יְלַמְּדוּ עֲלֵיהֶם וְעָלֵינוּ זְכוּת שֶׁתְּהֵא לְמִשְׁמֶרֶת שָׁלוֹם. וְנִשָּׂא בְרָכָה מֵאֵת יְיָ, וּצְדָקָה מֵאֱלֹהֵי יִשְׁעֵנוּ, וְנִמְצָא חֵן וְשֵׂכֶל טוֹב בְּעֵינֵי אֱלֹהִים וְאָדָם.

Ba'marom yilamdoo alay'hem v'alaynoo. Zchoot she't'hay lemishmeret shalom, ve'neesah v'racha may'ayt Adonoi, ootz'daka may'lohai yish'aynoo, ve'nimtzah chayn vesaychel tov b'aynai Eloheem v'adam.

In the high place, may they teach about them and about us, merit that will be protection of peace, and may we carry a blessing from Adonoi and righteousness from the God of our salvation, and may we find grace and good understanding in the eyes of God and humanity.

בְּשַׁבָּת: הָרַחֲמָן הוּא יַנְחִילֵנוּ יוֹם שֶׁכֻּלוֹ שַׁבָּת וּמְנוּחָה לְחַיֵּי הָעוֹלָמִים.

On Shabbat: Ha'rachaman hoo yan'chee'laynoo yom she'koolo Shabbat oo'menucha l'chayay ha'olameem.

[On Shabbat, add: May the Compassionate One bequeath to us a day that will be completely Shabbat and rest for eternal life.]

הָרַחֲמָן הוּא יַנְחִילֵנוּ יוֹם שֶׁכֻּלוֹ טוֹב.

הָרַחֲמָן הוּא יְזַכֵּנוּ לִימוֹת הַמָּשִׁיחַ וּלְחַיֵּי הָעוֹלָם הַבָּא.

Ha'rachaman hoo yancheelaynu yom she'koolo tov.

Harachaman hoo ye'zakaynoo lee'mot hamashee'ach oo'lecha'yay ha'olam haba.

May the Compassionate One bequeath us a day that is all good.

May the Compassionate One give us merit for the days of the messiah and for the life of the world to come.

מִגְדּוֹל יְשׁוּעוֹת מַלְכּוֹ וְעֹשֶׂה חֶסֶד לִמְשִׁיחוֹ לְדָוִד וּלְזַרְעוֹ עַד עוֹלָם.

Migdol yeshoo'ot malko ve'oseh chased limsheecho, l'Daveed oo'le'zar'o ad olam.

A tower of salvations is our Ruler, God does lovingkindness with God's anointed one, for David and his offspring, forever [II Samuel 22:51].

עֹשֶׂה שָׁלוֹם בִּמְרוֹמָיו, הוּא יַעֲשֶׂה שָׁלוֹם עָלֵינוּ וְעַל כָּל יִשְׂרָאֵל וְאִמְרוּ, אָמֵן.

Oseh shalom bim'ro'mav, hoo ya'aseh shalom alaynoo v'al kol Yisrael v'im'roo amayn.

May the One who makes peace in God's high places make peace upon us and upon all of Israel; and say, Amen.

יִרְאוּ אֶת יְיָ קְדֹשָׁיו, כִּי אֵין מַחְסוֹר לִירֵאָיו.

כְּפִירִים רָשׁוּ וְרָעֵבוּ, וְדֹרְשֵׁי יְיָ לֹא יַחְסְרוּ כָל טוֹב.

Yir'oo et Adonoi, kedoshav, kee ayn machzor lee'rayov.

K'feereem rashu, v'ra'ayvoo, vedorshay Adonoi lo yach'seroo kol tov.

May God's holy ones fear Adonoi, since there is no lack for those that fear God.

Young lions may go without and hunger, but seekers of Adonoi will not lack any good [Psalm 34:10–11].

הוֹדוּ לַיְיָ כִּי טוֹב כִּי לְעוֹלָם חַסְדּוֹ.

Hodoo la'donoi kee tov, kee l'olam chasdo.

Thank Adonoi, for God is good, since God's lovingkindness is forever [Psalm 118:1].

פּוֹתֵחַ אֶת יָדֶךָ, וּמַשְׂבִּיעַ לְכָל חַי רָצוֹן.

Potayach et yadecha, oo'masb'bee'a l'chol chai ratzon.

You open Your hand and satisfy the will of all living things [Psalm 146:16].

בָּרוּךְ הַגֶּבֶר אֲשֶׁר יִבְטַח בַּיְיָ, וְהָיָה יְיָ מִבְטַחוֹ.

Baruch ha'gever asher yivtach bA'donoi, vehaya Adonoi mivtacho.

Blessed is the one that will trust in Adonoi and Adonoi will be his security [Jeremiah 17:7].

נַעַר הָיִיתִי גַם זָקַנְתִּי, וְלֹא רָאִיתִי צַדִּיק נֶעֱזָב, וְזַרְעוֹ מְבַקֶּשׁ לָחֶם.

Na'ar hayeetee, gam zakantee, ve'lo ra'eetee tzadeek ne'ezav, ve'zar'o mevakesh lachem.

I was a youth and I have also aged and I have not seen a righteous man abandoned and his children seeking bread [Psalm 37:25].

יְיָ עֹז לְעַמּוֹ יִתֵּן, יְיָ יְבָרֵךְ אֶת עַמּוֹ בַשָּׁלוֹם.

Adonoi oz le'amo yeetayn, Adonoi yevaraych et amo vashalom.

Adonoi will give strength to God's people. Adonoi will bless God's people with peace [Psalm 29:11].

IF YOU'VE STILL GOT YOUR
WITS ABOUT YOU, OR EVEN IF YOU DON'T,
THE THIRD CUP OF WINE IS FILLED NOW
AND MEANT TO BE CONSUMED
AFTER SAYING THE FOLLOWING:

בָּרוּךְ אַתָּה יְיָ, אֱלֹהֵינוּ מֶלֶךְ הָעוֹלָם, בּוֹרֵא פְּרִי הַגָּפֶן.

Baruch ata Adonoi, Elohaynoo melech ha'olam, boray p'ree hagafen.

Blessed are You, Adonoi our God, Ruler of the Universe, who creates the fruit of the vine.

DRINK THE THIRD CUP AND POUR THE
FOURTH CUP. IF YOU HAVEN'T YET POURED
ELIJAH'S CUP (SOME KEEP IT ON THE TABLE
FOR THE WHOLE NIGHT), DO IT NOW.

Elijah's Cup

Singer/songwriter Laura Nyro tipped us off: **"Eli's Coming."** 🎵 On every Pesach table, a fifth cup of wine sits untouched, poured for the prophet Elijah, who is supposed to show up one day heralding the arrival of the Messiah. At the very end of the Seder, we open the door to welcome him. It's also symbolic of our trust in God's protection, since doorways play a role in the story of Pesach—**"Blood of the Lamb"** 🎵 on the doorpost and all.

Committed to God with absolute conviction, Elijah is an intense dude, a proselytizer for Jews who've strayed from the faith, a **"Tubthumper"** 🎵 like Chumbawamba sang about. He's even too much for God sometimes, leading to the possibly apocryphal tale that God once actually fired him, making him the only prophet ever to be fired. He's also a shape-shifter, kind of like a Marvel omnimorph, and he uses this superpower to help people who are in trouble. When his spectacular life comes to an end, he rides off in a chariot of fire.

Van Halen front man David Lee Roth has said he was envisioning a Jewish rock 'n' roll superhero when he created his wild, high-jumping stage persona, because he felt there weren't any Jewish superheroes. But the folklore around Elijah makes him sound like a superhero. What else would be expected from a prophet heralding the arrival of the Messiah? Maybe the song we sing to welcome him is intended to keep him calm. It's definitely why his cup of wine is already poured; in case he turns up, we don't want to keep him waiting.

The host, and/or anyone who wants to, now rises and opens the front door, and everyone sings (or recites) the following:

אֵלִיָּהוּ הַנָּבִיא, אֵלִיָּהוּ הַתִּשְׁבִּי, אֵלִיָּהוּ הַגִּלְעָדִי
בִּמְהֵרָה יָבוֹא אֵלֵינוּ עִם מָשִׁיחַ בֶּן דָּוִד.

Aylee'yahoo ha'navee, Aylee'yahoo ha'Tishbee, Eleeyahoo ha'Giladee,

Bim'hayra v'yamaynoo, yavo aylaynoo, im mashee'ach ben Daveed.

Elijah the Prophet, Elijah the Tishbi, Elijah the Giladi,

Speedily in our day may come to us, with Mashiach the son of David.

In her song "Eli's Coming," Laura Nyro warns of the consequences of temptation, echoing the story of Elijah the prophet and his warnings to the Jewish people about straying from our faith.

Hallel: הַלֵּל Coda

Some Seders include a reading of Psalms 115–18 at this juncture. This may be done uproariously together, or quietly to oneself. The words are below. Or sing along with Leonard Cohen's **"Hallelujah."** 🎼

Psalm 115

לֹא לָנוּ, יְיָ, לֹא לָנוּ, כִּי לְשִׁמְךָ תֵּן כָּבוֹד, עַל חַסְדְּךָ עַל אֲמִתֶּךָ.

לָמָּה יֹאמְרוּ הַגּוֹיִם אַיֵּה נָא אֱלֹהֵיהֶם.

וֵאלֹהֵינוּ בַשָּׁמַיִם, כֹּל אֲשֶׁר חָפֵץ עָשָׂה.

עֲצַבֵּיהֶם כֶּסֶף וְזָהָב מַעֲשֵׂה יְדֵי אָדָם.

פֶּה לָהֶם וְלֹא יְדַבֵּרוּ, עֵינַיִם לָהֶם וְלֹא יִרְאוּ.

אָזְנַיִם לָהֶם וְלֹא יִשְׁמָעוּ, אַף לָהֶם וְלֹא יְרִיחוּן.

יְדֵיהֶם וְלֹא יְמִישׁוּן, רַגְלֵיהֶם וְלֹא יְהַלֵּכוּ, לֹא יֶהְגּוּ בִּגְרוֹנָם.

כְּמוֹהֶם יִהְיוּ עֹשֵׂיהֶם, כֹּל אֲשֶׁר בֹּטֵחַ בָּהֶם.

יִשְׂרָאֵל בְּטַח בַּיָי, עֶזְרָם וּמָגִנָּם הוּא.

בֵּית אַהֲרֹן בִּטְחוּ בַיָי, עֶזְרָם וּמָגִנָּם הוּא.

יִרְאֵי יְיָ בִּטְחוּ בַיָי, עֶזְרָם וּמָגִנָּם הוּא.

יְיָ זְכָרָנוּ יְבָרֵךְ.

יְבָרֵךְ אֶת בֵּית יִשְׂרָאֵל, יְבָרֵךְ אֶת בֵּית אַהֲרֹן, יְבָרֵךְ יִרְאֵי יְיָ, הַקְּטַנִּים עִם הַגְּדֹלִים.

יֹסֵף יְיָ עֲלֵיכֶם, עֲלֵיכֶם וְעַל בְּנֵיכֶם. בְּרוּכִים אַתֶּם לַיָי, עֹשֵׂה שָׁמַיִם וָאָרֶץ.

הַשָּׁמַיִם שָׁמַיִם לַיָי וְהָאָרֶץ נָתַן לִבְנֵי אָדָם.

לֹא הַמֵּתִים יְהַלְלוּ יָהּ וְלֹא כָּל יֹרְדֵי דוּמָה.

וַאֲנַחְנוּ נְבָרֵךְ יָהּ מֵעַתָּה וְעַד עוֹלָם. הַלְלוּיָהּ.

Hallelujah! Leonard Cohen Turns the Seder Upside Down

Deeply philosophical, darkly auraed, and infinitely spiritual, Leonard Cohen was a poet/novelist before he stepped into the folk-rock scene of the 1960s and 1970s and took his place next to some of the greatest songwriters of that era. He's one of the few writers whose lyrics are true poetry, pondering vast, impossible questions via themes of melancholia, desire, God, and loss.

After living on the bohemian Greek island of Hydra for seven years, he landed in Los Angeles and gave his song **"Suzanne"** to Judy Collins, catapulting himself into a spotlight he wasn't totally prepared for. He dropped acid and charmed countless women, famous and not. He dallied on the periphery of the Velvet Underground and Andy Warhol's Factory. For decades, he remained an unusual figure in counterculture: religious, mysterious, and ever clad in a suit, tie, and fedora.

Raised in Quebec in an erudite Orthodox family, Cohen remained aligned with Judaism throughout his life, which for him meant lighting Shabbat candles on tour, among other things. In 1994, he ascended the Mt. Baldy Zen Center in Southern California's San Gabriel Mountains, stayed for five years, and emerged an ordained Rinzai Zen Buddhist monk. Many, including fellow poet Allen Ginsberg, asked how he reconciled belonging to two faiths. "Well, for one thing, in the tradition of Zen that I've practiced, there is no prayerful worship and there is no affirmation of a deity," Cohen said. "So theologically there is no challenge to any Jewish belief." He called Buddhism a "tuning fork for consciousness" and credited it for helping him let go of worry and control. "The older I get, the surer I am that I'm not running the show," he says.

On an endless quest for enlightenment, he was drawn to spiritual leaders. He spent part of the late 1990s living in Mumbai to study with Advaita guru Ramesh Balsekar. In the last decade of his life (Cohen died in 2016), he joined the congregation of Rabbi Mordecai Finley, founder of Ohr HaTorah Synagogue in Los Angeles.

Invited to the rabbi's home for a Passover Seder, Cohen brought Eastern practices to the proceedings. "He testified to the benefits of yoga and showed us poses, including standing on his head," Rabbi Finley says. The mind/body practice isn't as out of place at the Seder as it may sound. For those who recite Hallel after the festive meal with all the joy and vigor that's supposed to accompany those psalms, a little stretch and warm-up is a good idea. If anyone understood this, it would've been Cohen. His best-known song is **"Hallelujah,"** a prana-channeling dirge that slowly builds in intensity. The word, an expression of rejoicing and praising God, appears many times in the Psalms and gives Hallel its name. "It's a desire to affirm my faith in life, not in some formal religious way, but with enthusiasm, with emotion," he said.

Cohen and his rabbi shared an interest in Lurianic Kabbalah, which they studied together. Based on the work of brilliant Talmudic scholar, mystic, and poet Rabbi Isaac ben Solomon Luria, it centered on three main themes: tzimtzum (contraction), shevirat ha-kelim (the shattering of the vessels), and tikkun (repair or fixing). Cohen had difficulty accepting that tikkun was possible. "He said to me that the human condition is mangled into a box into which the broken soul does not fit," Findley says. Yet on songs like 1992's **"Anthem,"** the man known as the Poet of Brokenness focuses on the light that shines through the cracks.

131

Rock Photographer
Bob Gruen Welcomes Elijah

Growing up in New York, Bob Gruen's favorite part of his family's Seder was getting up and opening the door for Elijah. It was a chance to stretch his legs during the long night of sitting at a table, and "hang out and get some fresh air for a little while," he says. "It's also a dramatic thing, to open the door and call out to Elijah." Assigned the part of Elijah at a City Winery Seder decades later, Gruen compared him to John Lennon and Yoko Ono, Patti Smith, Bob Dylan, and Joe Strummer. "They were all prophets of truth, spreading the word to the people," he says.

Gruen is one of rock 'n' roll's most renowned photographers, having created iconic images such as John Lennon in the New York City T-shirt and Led Zeppelin standing beside the wing of their private jet. His work took him around the world, shooting everyone from Les Paul to Lady Gaga. Wherever he'd land on any given Passover, he'd seek out a Seder. On a junket to Tokyo with KISS, Gruen accepted an invitation to a Seder and dressed up in a fitted vintage suit. "Gene Simmons looked at me and said, 'That's the suit I got beat up for wearing when I was a kid going to Hebrew school,'" he says with a laugh.

For years, an annual Pesach tradition for Gruen was a gathering of friends from New York's 1970s downtown club scene at the Gramercy Park home of designer Abbijane Schifrin. Known professionally by her mononym, Abbijane owned a brownstone on a section of East Nineteenth Street known as Block Beautiful. Her eclectic decor—brightly painted rooms and vintage furnishings—earned it a distinctive moniker: the Technicolor Townhouse. She held imaginative fashion shows there to present her couture collections.

On Passover, Abbijane hosted Gruen and other downtown doyens who'd met at long-gone clubs like Max's Kansas City, the Mercer Arts Center, and the Mudd Club (and CBGB, which took its final bow in 2006). The 1970s had been a wildly creative period in New York for aspiring musicians, fashion designers, and artists of all sorts. Through his photographs, Gruen documented this cultural revolution in real time, and the long tail of its influence ever since.

Guests included Lenny Kaye, the musician/writer/producer responsible for the *Nuggets* compilations, highly influential anthologies of 1960s garage rock, and a longtime collaborator of Patti Smith. Hal Willner was a regular, as was CBS Records head Walter Yetnikoff, who co-owned the building with Abbijane for a time. Known for overseeing successes of artists like Bruce Springsteen and Gloria Estefan, Yetnikoff also pressed MTV to add Michael Jackson videos to their early rotation, and pried Billy Joel's music publishing from the hands of Joel's former manager, delivering them back to the artist. Phyllis Stein, scenester and former girlfriend of New York Dolls drummer Jerry Nolan, brought her little daughter, Courtney, who'd ask the Four Questions.

"We all had the traditional upbringing, but Lenny and me were the most sentimental, trying to revive some of our youthful memories and have a real Seder," Gruen says. "We felt the necessity to repeat the story the way we're supposed to. We managed to sing a couple of the old songs at the end, too. For me, it was just tradition. For Lenny—he could actually sing!" The customary food was something Gruen looked forward to all year. "We'd have lamb shank, charoset, matzah ball soup—tastes you only get that night," he says. "The sweetness and the sourness of charoset, the horseradish—that's really my favorite part of the meal. That and the wine."

Rather than simply opening the front door for Elijah, Abbijane and her guests welcomed in the sounds of the Brotherhood Synagogue adjacent to her property. "We would leave the doors open, and we could hear the services across the backyard," Gruen says. Built as a Quaker meeting house in 1859, the location was a stop on the Underground Railroad in its early years.

Abbijane passed away in 2009, and as others in the friend group left New York it became more difficult to maintain the annual tradition. Passover remains Gruen's favorite holiday, though. "Passover is all about freedom, and freedom has been the theme of my life," he says. "My work with rock 'n' roll is about freedom. For me, rock 'n' roll is the freedom to express your feelings very loudly in public. The feeling I'm trying to capture in my photographs, it's not just about a pop star portrait, it's the feeling that pop star is putting out. And that feeling is freedom."

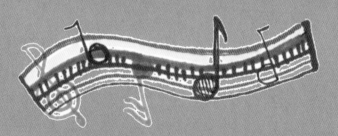

Lo lanoo Adonoi lo lanoo kee le'shimcha tayn kavod; al chas'de'cha al ameetecha.

Lamah yo'me'roo ha'goyeem a'yay na elohayhem.

Vay'lo'haynoo vasha'mayeem kol asher chafetz asah.

Atza'bayhem kesef ve'zahav; ma'a'say yeday adam.

Peh lahem ve'lo ye'dab'roo; aynayim lahem ve'lo yir'oo.

Oz'nayeem lahem ve'lo yish'ma'oo; af lahem ve'lo ye'ree'choon.

Yedayhem ve'lo yemee'shoon rag'layhem ve'lo ye'ha'lay'choo; lo yeh'g'oo bi'gronam.

Kemo'hem yihee'yoo osayhem; kol asher botayach bahem.

Yisrael betach b'Adonoi, ezram oo'mageenam hoo.

Bayt Aharon bitchoo v'Adonoi, ezram oo'magenam hoo.

Yir'ay Adonoi bit'choo b'Adonoi ezram oo'mageenam hoo.

Adonoi zecharanoo, yevaraych et bayt yisra'ayl; ye'va'raych et bayt Aharon.

Yevaraych yir'ay Adonoi, ha'ketaneem im ha'gedoleem.

Yosayf Adonoi alaychem, alaychem v'al b'naychem.

Beroocheem atem l'Adonoi, oseh shamayim va'aretz.

Hashamayeem shamayim l'Adonoi, ve'ha'aretz natan liv'nay adam.

Lo hamayteem yi'haleloo Yah, velo chol yorday doomah.

Va'a'nachnoo nevaraych Yah, may'atah v'ad olam halelooyah.

Not for us, not for us, but rather for Your name, give glory for your kindness and for your truth.

Why will the nations say, "Where is their God?"

But our God is in the heavens; all that God wanted, God did.

Their idols are silver and gold, the work of human hands.

They have a mouth but will not speak; they have eyes but will not see.

They have ears but will not hear; they have a nose but will not smell.

Their hands, but they will not feel; their feet, but will not walk;

they will not make a sound from their throat.

Like them will be their makers, all who trust in them.

Israel, trust in Adonoi; God is their help and their shield.

House of Aaron, trust in Adonoi; God is their help and their shield.

Those that fear Adonoi, trust in Adonoi; God is their help and their shield.

May Adonoi who remembers us, bless;

May God bless the House of Israel; May God bless the House of Aaron.

May God bless those that fear Adonoi, the small ones with the great ones.

May Adonoi bring increase to you, to you and for your children.

Blessed are you to Adonoi, the maker of the heavens and the earth.

The heavens are heavens for Adonoi, but the earth God gave to humankind.

The dead will not praise Adonoi, nor will all those that go down to silence.

But we will bless Adonoi from now and forever. Halleluyah!

Psalm 116:1–11

אָהַבְתִּי כִּי יִשְׁמַע יְיָ אֶת קוֹלִי תַּחֲנוּנָי. כִּי הִטָּה אָזְנוֹ
לִי וּבְיָמַי אֶקְרָא.

אֲפָפוּנִי חֶבְלֵי מָוֶת וּמְצָרֵי שְׁאוֹל מְצָאוּנִי, צָרָה וְיָגוֹן
אֶמְצָא.

וּבְשֵׁם יְיָ אֶקְרָא: אָנָּא יְיָ מַלְּטָה נַפְשִׁי.

חַנּוּן יְיָ וְצַדִּיק, וֵאלֹהֵינוּ מְרַחֵם. שֹׁמֵר פְּתָאִים יְיָ,
דַּלּוֹתִי וְלִי יְהוֹשִׁיעַ.

שׁוּבִי נַפְשִׁי לִמְנוּחָיְכִי, כִּי יְיָ גָּמַל עָלָיְכִי.

כִּי חִלַּצְתָּ נַפְשִׁי מִמָּוֶת, אֶת עֵינִי מִן דִּמְעָה, אֶת
רַגְלִי מִדֶּחִי.

אֶתְהַלֵּךְ לִפְנֵי יְיָ בְּאַרְצוֹת הַחַיִּים. הֶאֱמַנְתִּי כִּי
אֲדַבֵּר, אֲנִי עָנִיתִי מְאֹד.

אֲנִי אָמַרְתִּי בְחָפְזִי כָּל הָאָדָם כֹּזֵב.

Ahavtee kee yishmah Adonoi et kolee tacha'noonee.

Kee hee'tah oz'nav lee oo'veyamai ekra.

Afafoonee chavlay mavet oo'metzaray sheol meta'oonee. Tzarah ve'yagon emtza.

Oo've'shaym Adonoi ekra; ana Adonoi mal'tah nafshee.

Chanoon Adonoi ve'tzadeek, vaylo-haynoo merachaym.

Shomayr petayeem Adonoi, dalotee ve'lee yehosheea.

Shoovee nafshaa lim'noo'chai'chee, kee Adonoi gamal a'lai'yechee.

Kee cheelatz'ta nafshee mee'ma'vet et aynai meedim'ah et raglee mee'dechee.

Et'ha'laych lifnay Adonoi, be'artzot ha'cha'yeem.

He'emantee kee daber, anee aneetee me'od.

Anee amartee ve'chof'zee kol ha'adam kozayv.

I have loved Adonoi, for God hears my voice, my pleas.

For God inclined God's ear to me— and in my days, I will call out.

The pangs of death have encircled me and the straits of Sheol have found me

and I have found trouble and sorrow.

And I will call the name of Adonoi, "Please, Adonoi, rescue my soul."

Gracious is Adonoi and righteous, and our God is compassionate.

Adonoi watches over the simple; I was poor and God saved me.

Return, my soul, to your tranquility, since Adonoi has favored you.

For You have rescued my soul from death, my eyes from tears, my feet from stumbling.

I will walk before Adonoi in the lands of the living.

I have trusted; when I speak, I am very afflicted.

I said in my haste, all men are false.

Psalm 116:12–19

מָה אָשִׁיב לַיְיָ כָּל תַּגְמוּלוֹהִי עָלָי. כּוֹס יְשׁוּעוֹת
אֶשָּׂא וּבְשֵׁם יְיָ אֶקְרָא.

נְדָרַי לַיְיָ אֲשַׁלֵּם נֶגְדָה נָּא לְכָל עַמּוֹ.

יָקָר בְּעֵינֵי יְיָ הַמָּוְתָה לַחֲסִידָיו.

אָנָּה יְיָ כִּי אֲנִי עַבְדֶּךָ, אֲנִי עַבְדְּךָ בֶּן אֲמָתֶךָ, פִּתַּחְתָּ
לְמוֹסֵרָי.

לְךָ אֶזְבַּח זֶבַח תּוֹדָה וּבְשֵׁם יְיָ אֶקְרָא. נְדָרַי לַיְיָ
אֲשַׁלֵּם נֶגְדָה נָּא לְכָל עַמּוֹ.

בְּחַצְרוֹת בֵּית יְיָ, בְּתוֹכֵכִי יְרוּשָׁלַיִם. הַלְלוּיָהּ.

Mah asheev la'donoi, kol
tag'moo'low'hee alai.

Kos yeshoo'ot esa, oo'v'shaym
Adonoi ekra.

Nedarai la'donoi ashalaym, negda'na
le'chol amov.

Yakar b'aynai Adonoi ha'mav'ta
la'cha'see'dav.

Ana Adonoi kee ani avdecha ani
avdecha ben ama'techa; pee'tachta
le'mosrai.

Lecha ezbach zevach todah,
oo'v'shaym Adonoi ekra.

Nedarai l'Adonoi ashalaym negday
l'chol amav.

Bechatzrot bayt Adonoi betoche'chi
Yeroosha'layeem. Halayluyah!

What can I return to Adonoi for all
that God has favored me?

A cup of salvations I will lift and I will
call out in the name of Adonoi.

My vows to Adonoi I will pay, in front
of God's entire people.

Precious in the eyes of Adonoi is the
death of God's pious ones.

Please, Adonoi, for I am Your servant,
the son of Your maidservant; You
have opened my bonds. To You I will
offer a thanksgiving offering and I will
call out in the name of Adonoi.

My vows to Adonoi I will pay, in front
of God's people.

In the courtyards of the house of
Adonoi, in your midst, Jerusalem.
Halleluyah!

Psalm 117–18:4

הַלְלוּ אֶת יְיָ כָּל גּוֹיִם, שַׁבְּחוּהוּ כָּל הָאֻמִּים.

כִּי גָבַר עָלֵינוּ חַסְדּוֹ, וֶאֱמֶת יְיָ לְעוֹלָם. הַלְלוּיָהּ.

הוֹדוּ לַיְיָ כִּי טוֹב כִּי לְעוֹלָם חַסְדּוֹ.

יֹאמַר נָא יִשְׂרָאֵל כִּי לְעוֹלָם חַסְדּוֹ.

יֹאמְרוּ נָא בֵית אַהֲרֹן כִּי לְעוֹלָם חַסְדּוֹ.

יֹאמְרוּ נָא יִרְאֵי יְיָ כִּי לְעוֹלָם חַסְדּוֹ.

Hal'le'loo et Adonoi ko goyeem,
shab'choo'hoo kol ha'oomeem.

Kee gavar alaynoo chasdo ve'emet
Adonoi l'olam ha'le'loo'yah.

Ho'doo l'Adonoi, kee tov, kee l'olam
chasdo.

Yomar na Yisra'el, kee l'olam chasdo.

Yom'roo na, vayt Aharon, kee l'olam
chasdo.

Yom'roo na, yir'ay Adonoi, kee l'olam
chasdo.

Praise Adonoi, all nations; extol God
all the peoples.

For God's lovingkindness has
overpowered and the truth of
Adonoi is forever. Halleluyah! Thank
Adonoi, for God is good, since God's
lovingkindness is forever.

Let Israel say, Give thanks to
Adonoi, for God is good, for God's
lovingkindness is forever.

Let the House of Aaron say,

Give thanks to Adonoi, for God is
good, for God's lovingkindness is
forever.

Let those that fear Adonoi say,

Give thanks to Adonoi, for God is
good, for God's lovingkindness is
forever.

Psalm 118:5–20

מִן הַמֵּצַר קָרָאתִי יָהּ, עָנָנִי בַמֶּרְחַב יָהּ.

יְיָ לִי, לֹא אִירָא – מַה יַּעֲשֶׂה לִי אָדָם, יְיָ לִי בְּעֹזְרָי וַאֲנִי אֶרְאֶה בְשֹׂנְאָי.

טוֹב לַחֲסוֹת בַּיְיָ מִבְּטֹחַ בָּאָדָם. טוֹב לַחֲסוֹת בַּיְיָ מִבְּטֹחַ בִּנְדִיבִים.

כָּל גּוֹיִם סְבָבוּנִי, בְּשֵׁם יְיָ כִּי אֲמִילַם. סַבּוּנִי גַם סְבָבוּנִי, בְּשֵׁם יְיָ כִּי אֲמִילַם.

סַבּוּנִי כִדְבֹרִים, דֹּעֲכוּ כְּאֵשׁ קוֹצִים, בְּשֵׁם ה' כִּי אֲמִילַם.

דָּחֹה דְחִיתַנִי לִנְפֹּל, וַיְיָ עֲזָרָנִי. עָזִּי וְזִמְרָת יָהּ וַיְהִי לִי לִישׁוּעָה.

קוֹל רִנָּה וִישׁוּעָה בְּאָהֳלֵי צַדִּיקִים:

יְמִין יְיָ עֹשָׂה חָיִל, יְמִין ה' רוֹמֵמָה, יְמִין יְיָ עֹשָׂה חָיִל.

לֹא אָמוּת כִּי אֶחְיֶה, וַאֲסַפֵּר מַעֲשֵׂי יָהּ. יַסֹּר יִסְּרַנִי יָהּ, וְלַמָּוֶת לֹא נְתָנָנִי.

פִּתְחוּ לִי שַׁעֲרֵי צֶדֶק, אָבֹא בָם, אוֹדֶה יָהּ. זֶה הַשַּׁעַר לַיְיָ, צַדִּיקִים יָבֹאוּ בוֹ.

Min ha'maytzar ka'ra'tee Yah, a'nanee va'merchav Yah.

Adonoi lee lo eera, mah ya'a'seh lee a'dam.

Adonoi lee be'oze'rai, va'a'nee er'eh ve'sone'ai.

Tov la'cha'sot b'Adonoi, mee'b'to'ach ba'a'dam.

Tov la'cha'sot b'Adonoi, mee'b'to'ach bin'dee'veem.

Kol go'yeem se'va'voo'nee, be'shaym Adonoi kee amee'lam.

Sa'boo'nee gam seva'voonee, be'shaym Adonoi kee amee'lam.

Sa'boo'nee chid'voe'reem doe'a'choo ke'aysh koe'tzeem, be'shaym Adonoi kee amee'lam.

Da'choe de'chee'ta'nee lin'pole, Va'donoi a'za'ra'nee.

Ozee v'zim'rat Yah, va'yehee lee lee'shoo'ah.

Kol reenah ve'shoo'ah b'aw'haw'lay tza'deekeem, ye'meen Adonoi o'sah cha'yil.

Yee·meen Adonoi ro'me'mah, ye'meen Adonoi o'sah cha'yil.

Lo amoot kee ech'yeh, va'a'sa'pair ma'a'say Yah.

Ya'sore yis'ranee Yah ve'la'mavet lo ne'ta'nani.

Pitchoo lee sha'a'ray tzedek, avo'vam odeh Yah.

Zeh ha'sha'ar l'Adonoi, tza'deekeem ya'vo'oo voe.

From the narrow place I have called Yah, God answered me in the wide space of Yah.

Adonoi is for me, I will not fear, what will a person do to me?

Adonoi is for me with my helpers, and I shall see my enemies.

It is better to take shelter in Adonoi than to trust in a person.

It is better to take shelter in Adonoi than to trust in nobles.

All the nations surrounded me; in the name of Adonoi I will destroy them.

They surrounded me, they also encircled me; in the name of Adonoi I will destroy them.

They surrounded me like bees, they died out like a fire of thorns;

In the name of Adonoi I will destroy them.

You have surely pushed me to fall, but Adonoi helped me.

The strength and might of Yah have become salvation for me.

The sound of happy song and salvation is in the tents of the righteous.

The right hand of Adonoi acts powerfully!

The right hand of Adonoi is exalted! The right hand of Adonoi acts powerfully!

I will not die, for I will live and I will tell the deeds of Adonoi.

Adonoi has surely punished me, but has not given me to death.

Open up for me the gates of righteousness; I will enter them, and I will thank Adonoi.

This is the gate to Adonoi; righteous will enter it.

Psalm 118:21–24

אוֹדְךָ כִּי עֲנִיתָנִי וַתְּהִי לִי לִישׁוּעָה.

אֶבֶן מָאֲסוּ הַבּוֹנִים הָיְתָה לְרֹאשׁ פִּנָּה.

מֵאֵת יְיָ הָיְתָה זֹּאת הִיא נִפְלָאת בְּעֵינֵינוּ.

זֶה הַיּוֹם עָשָׂה יְיָ נָגִילָה וְנִשְׂמְחָה בוֹ.

Ode'cha kee Aneeta lee, va'tehee lee leeshoo'a.

Even ma'asoo habonim, hai'ta l'rosh peena.

May'ayt Adonoi ha'yeta zot hee niflat b'ay'nay'noo.

Zeh hayom asah Adonoi, nageela v'nis'm'cha vo.

I will thank You, for You answered me and You have become salvation for me.

A stone that was rejected by the builders has become the chief cornerstone.

From Adonoi was this; it is wondrous in our eyes.

This is the day Adonoi made; let us rejoice and be happy in it.

Psalm 118:25

אָנָּא יְיָ, הוֹשִׁיעָה נָּא. אָנָּא יְיָ, הוֹשִׁיעָה נָּא. אָנָּא יְיָ, הַצְלִיחָה נָא. אָנָּא יְיָ, הַצְלִיחָה נָא.

Ana Adonoi, ho'shee'a na. Ana Adonoi, ho'shee'a na.

Ana Adonoi, hatz'lee'cha na. Ana Adonoi, hatz'lee'cha'na.

Please, Adonoi, save us! Please, Adonoi, save us!

Please, Adonoi, give us success! Please, Adonoi, give us success!

Psalm 118:26–29

בָּרוּךְ הַבָּא בְּשֵׁם יְיָ, בֵּרַכְנוּכֶם מִבֵּית יְיָ. בָּרוּךְ הַבָּא בְּשֵׁם יְיָ, בֵּרַכְנוּכֶם מִבֵּית יְיָ.

אֵל יְיָ וַיָּאֶר לָנוּ. אִסְרוּ חַג בַּעֲבֹתִים עַד קַרְנוֹת הַמִּזְ־בֵּחַ.

אֵל יְיָ וַיָּאֶר לָנוּ. אִסְרוּ חַג בַּעֲבֹתִים עַד קַרְנוֹת הַמִּזְ־בֵּחַ.

אֵלִי אַתָּה וְאוֹדֶךָּ, אֱלֹהַי – אֲרוֹמְמֶךָּ. אֵלִי אַתָּה וְאוֹדֶךָּ, אֱלֹהַי – אֲרוֹמְמֶךָּ.

הוֹדוּ לַיְיָ כִּי טוֹב, כִּי לְעוֹלָם חַסְדּוֹ. הוֹדוּ לַיְיָ כִּי טוֹב, כִּי לְעוֹלָם חַסְדּוֹ.

Ba'ruch ha'ba b'shaym Adonoi, bay'rach'noo'chem mee'bayt Adonoi.

Ba'ruch ha'ba b'shaym Adonoi, bay'rach'noo'chem mee'bayt Adonoi.

El Adonoi va'ya'ayr lanoo, is'roo chag ba'avo'teem, ad kar'note ha'miz'bayach.

El Adonoi va'ya'ayr lanoo, is'roo chag ba'avo'teem, ad kar'note ha'miz'bayach.

Aylee atah ve'o'deka, e'lo'hai a'ro'm'meka. Aylee atah ve'o'deka, e'lo'hai a'ro'm'meka.

Hodoo la'Adonoi kee tov, kee l'olam chasdo. Hodoo la'Adonoi kee tov, kee l'olam chasdo.

Blessed be the one who comes in the name of Adonoi;

we have blessed you from the house of Adonoi.

God is Adonoi, and has illuminated us;

bind the festival offering with bonds to the corners of the altar.

You are my God and I will Thank You, my God and I will exalt You.

Thank Adonoi, for God is good, for God's lovingkindness is forever.

Yehaleloocha Adonoi Elohaynii kol ma'asecha, vachaseedecha tzadeekeem osay retzonecha, vechol amcha bayt Yisra'yl b'reena yodoo veevarchoo, vee'shabchoo vee'fa'aroo, vee'ro'me'moo ve'ya'a'retzoo, ve'yakdeeshoo, ve'yam'leechoo et shemecha, malkaynoo.

Kee lecha tov lehodot oo'leshimcha na'eh lezamayr, kee may'olam v'at olam atah ayl.

All your works will praise You, Adonoi our God,

And your pious ones, the righteous ones who do Your will, and all of Your people,

the House of Israel, with joyful song will thank and bless and praise and glorify,

and exalt and venerate, and sanctify and coronate Your name, our Ruler.

For to you it is good to thank, and to Your name it is fitting to sing,

For from always and eternally, you are God.

יְהַלְלוּךְ יְיָ אֱלֹהֵינוּ כָּל מַעֲשֶׂיךָ, וַחֲסִידֶיךָ צַדִּיקִים עוֹשֵׂי רְצוֹנֶךָ, וְכָל עַמְּךָ בֵּית יִשְׂרָאֵל בְּרִנָּה יוֹדוּ וִיבָרְכוּ, וִישַׁבְּחוּ וִיפָאֲרוּ, וִירוֹמְמוּ וְיַעֲרִיצוּ, וְיַקְדִּישׁוּ וְיַמְלִיכוּ אֶת שִׁמְךָ, מַלְכֵּנוּ.

כִּי לְךָ טוֹב לְהוֹדוֹת וּלְשִׁמְךָ נָאֶה לְזַמֵּר, כִּי מֵעוֹלָם וְעַד עוֹלָם אַתָּה אֵל.

READY TO DRINK THE FOURTH CUP?

SAY THE BRACHA FIRST:

בָּרוּךְ אַתָּה יְיָ, אֱלֹהֵינוּ מֶלֶךְ הָעוֹלָם, בּוֹרֵא פְּרִי הַגָּפֶן.

Baruch atah Adonoi, Elohaynoo melech ha'olam, boray p'ree ha'gafen.

Blessed are You, Adonoi our God, Ruler of the Universe, who creates the fruit of the vine.

Nirtzah: נִרְצָה
The Seder Concludes

Nirtzah means "acceptance," as in we hope our Seder has been accepted by God. It's an acknowledgment of the conclusion of the Seder. Traditionally, we end by saying "Next year in Jerusalem."

It's a phrase used by Jews in the Diaspora for more than a thousand years, and it's a reminder that we're still in exile. That's not to say that the **"Green, Green Grass of Home"** 🎵 isn't really your home, but, historically, this hasn't always worked out so well for us.

"Next year in Jerusalem" has been added to and taken out of Haggadahs for centuries, depending on what horrors or hopes surrounded the Jewish people at any given time. It can be literal, a prayer for the arrival of Moshiach. It can be a call for refuge, the concept that there's one place where Jews might be safe from another attempted annihilation. It can be a dream of a world without antisemitism, without hate; in other words, peace on earth.

לְשָׁנָה הַבָּאָה בִּירוּשָׁלָיִם!

L'SHANAH HA'BA'AH
B'YERUSHALAYIM!

NEXT YEAR IN JERUSALEM!

Everybody Sing!

Singing at the end of the Seder is a tradition that has evolved over centuries, and three songs in particular cap many a Pesach celebration: "Adir Hu," "Echad Mi Yodea," and "Chad Gadya." They may sound like kids' music, but each one contains considerable Jewish themes, philosophical musings, and Almighty praising.

"Mighty Is God" "אַדִּיר הוּא" "Adir Hu"

Most frequently sung in Hebrew (as the English translation is a bit clunky), "Adir Hu" or "Mighty Is God" may be traced back to the sixth or seventh century in what is now Germany. Set to a playful melody, it expresses the desire that Moshiach will arrive soon and rebuild the Holy Temple. It's an "alphabet" song—each word of praise starts with a letter of the Hebrew alphabet in order.

אַדִּיר הוּא יִבְנֶה בֵיתוֹ בְּקָרוֹב. בִּמְהֵרָה, בִּמְהֵרָה, בְּיָמֵינוּ בְּקָרוֹב. אֵל בְּנֵה, אֵל בְּנֵה, בְּנֵה בֵיתְךָ בְּקָרוֹב.

Adeer hoo, adeer hoo, yivneh bayto b'karov.

Bimhayra, bimhayra, b'yamaynoo b'karov.

Ayl b'nay, ayl b'nay, b'nay baytcha b'karov.

Mighty is God, may God build God's house soon. Quickly, quickly, in our days, soon.

God build, God build, build Your house soon.

בָּחוּר הוּא, גָּדוֹל הוּא, דָּגוּל הוּא יִבְנֶה בֵּיתוֹ

בְּקָרוֹב. בִּמְהֵרָה, בִּמְהֵרָה, בְּיָמֵינוּ בְּקָרוֹב. אֵל בְּנֵה, אֵל בְּנֵה, בְּנֵה בֵּיתְךָ בְּקָרוֹב.

Bachoor hoo, Gadol hoo, dagool hoo, yivneh bayto b'karov.

Bimhayra, bimhayra, b'yamaynoo b'karov.

Ayl b'nay, ayl b'nay, b'nay baytcha b'karov.

Chosen is God, great is God, outstanding is God. May God build God's house soon.

Quickly, quickly, in our days, soon. God build, God build, build Your house soon.

הָדוּר הוּא, וָתִיק הוּא, זַכַּאי הוּא יִבְנֶה בֵּיתוֹ בְּקָרוֹב. בִּמְהֵרָה, בִּמְהֵרָה, בְּיָמֵינוּ בְּקָרוֹב. אֵל בְּנֵה, אֵל בְּנֵה, בְּנֵה בֵיתְךָ בְּקָרוֹב.

Hadoor hoo, vateek hoo, zakkai hoo, yivneh bayto b'karov.

Bimhayra, bimhayra, b'yamaynoo b'karov.

Ayl b'nay, ayl b'nay, b'nay baytcha b'karov.

Splendid is God, ancient is God, worthy is God. May God build God's house soon.

Quickly, quickly, in our days, soon. God build, God build, build Your house soon.

חָסִיד הוּא, טָהוֹר הוּא, יָחִיד הוּא יִבְנֶה בֵּיתוֹ בְּקָרוֹב. בִּמְהֵרָה, בִּמְהֵרָה, בְּיָמֵינוּ בְּקָרוֹב. אֵל בְּנֵה, אֵל בְּנֵה, בְּנֵה בֵיתְךָ בְּקָרוֹב.

Chaseed hoo, tahor hoo, yacheed hoo, yivneh bayto b'karov.

Bimhayra, bimhayra, b'yamaynoo b'karov.

Ayl b'nay, ayl b'nay, b'nay baytcha b'karov.

Pious is God, pure is God, singular is God. May God build God's house soon.

Quickly, quickly, in our days, soon. God build, God build, build Your house soon.

כַּבִּיר הוּא, לָמוּד הוּא, מֶלֶךְ הוּא יִבְנֶה בֵּיתוֹ בְּקָרוֹב. בִּמְהֵרָה, בִּמְהֵרָה, בְּיָמֵינוּ בְּקָרוֹב. אֵל בְּנֵה, אֵל בְּנֵה, בְּנֵה בֵיתְךָ בְּקָרוֹב.

Kabeer hoo, lamood hoo, melech hoo, yivneh bayto b'karov.

Bimhayra, bimhayra, b'yamaynoo b'karov.

Ayl b'nay, ayl b'nay, b'nay baytcha b'karov.

Mighty is God, learned is God, sovereign is God. May God build God's house soon.

Quickly, quickly, in our days, soon. God build, God build, build Your house soon.

נוֹרָא הוּא, סַגִּיב הוּא, עִזּוּז הוּא יִבְנֶה בֵּיתוֹ בְּקָרוֹב. בִּמְהֵרָה, בִּמְהֵרָה, בְּיָמֵינוּ בְּקָרוֹב. אֵל בְּנֵה, אֵל בְּנֵה, בְּנֵה בֵיתְךָ בְּקָרוֹב.

Nora hoo, sageev hoo, eezooz hoo, yivneh bayto b'karov.

Bimhayra, bimhayra, b'yamaynoo b'karov.

Ayl b'nay, ayl b'nay, b'nay baytcha b'karov.

Awesome is God, mighty is God, powerful is God, may God build God's house soon.

Quickly, quickly, in our days, soon. God build, God build, build Your house soon.

פּוֹדֶה הוּא, צַדִּיק הוּא, קָדוֹשׁ הוּא יִבְנֶה בֵּיתוֹ בְּקָרוֹב. בִּמְהֵרָה, בִּמְהֵרָה, בְּיָמֵינוּ בְּקָרוֹב. אֵל בְּנֵה, אֵל בְּנֵה, בְּנֵה בֵיתְךָ בְּקָרוֹב.

Podeh hoo, tzadeek hoo, kadosh hoo, yivneh bayto b'karov.

Bimhayra, bimhayra, b'yamaynoo b'karov.

Ayl b'nay, ayl b'nay, b'nay baytcha b'karov.

A redeemer is God, righteous is God, holy is God. May God build God's house soon.

Quickly, quickly, in our days, soon. God build, God build, build Your house soon.

Rachoom hoo, Shaddai hoo, takeef hoo, yivneh bayto b'karov.

Bimhayra, bimhayra, b'yamaynoo b'karov.

Ayl b'nay, ayl b'nay, b'nay baytcha b'karov.

Compassionate is God, Shaddai is God, powerful is God. May God build God's house soon.

Quickly, quickly, in our days, soon. God build, God build, build Your house soon.

רַחוּם הוּא, שַׁדַּי הוּא, תַּקִּיף הוּא יִבְנֶה בֵּיתוֹ בְּקָרוֹב. בִּמְהֵרָה, בִּמְהֵרָה, בְּיָמֵינוּ בְּקָרוֹב. אֵל בְּנֵה, אֵל בְּנֵה, בְּנֵה בֵּיתְךָ בְּקָרוֹב.

"Who Knows One?"
"אֶחָד מִי יוֹדֵעַ?"
"Echad Mee Yodaya?"

This song is meant to keep kids awake until the end of the Seder. Evidently, keeping kids awake during Seders has been difficult for a long time; the origins of "Who Knows One?"/"Echad Mee Yodaya?" may date back to fifteenth-century Germany, and it seems to have made its first written appearance (along with "Chad Gadya") in the sixteenth-century Prague Haggadah. The song starts with the number one and builds up to thirteen, repeating every line as it goes along. Toward the conclusion, it's fun to see how fast everyone can sing without forgetting any of the words.

אֶחָד מִי יוֹדֵעַ? אֶחָד אֲנִי יוֹדֵעַ: אֶחָד אֱלֹהֵינוּ שֶׁבַּשָּׁמַיִם וּבָאָרֶץ.

Echad mee yodaya? Echad anee yodaya. Echad Elohaynoo she'bashamayim oova aretz.

Who knows one? I know one: One is our God who is in the heavens and the earth.

Shnai'yeem mee yodaya? Shnai'yeem anee yodaya. Shnay loochot ha'breet, echad Elohaynoo she'bashamayim oova'aretz.

Who knows two? I know two: Two tablets of the covenant.

One is our God who is in the heavens and the earth.

שְׁנַיִם מִי יוֹדֵעַ? שְׁנַיִם אֲנִי יוֹדֵעַ: שְׁנֵי לֻחוֹת הַבְּרִית. אֶחָד אֱלֹהֵינוּ שֶׁבַּשָּׁמַיִם וּבָאָרֶץ.

שְׁלֹשָׁה מִי יוֹדֵעַ? שְׁלֹשָׁה אֲנִי יוֹדֵעַ: שְׁלֹשָׁה אָבוֹת, שְׁנֵי לֻחוֹת הַבְּרִית, אֶחָד אֱלֹהֵינוּ שֶׁבַּשָּׁמַיִם וּבָאָרֶץ.

Shelosha mee yodaya? Shelosha anee yodaya. Shelosha avot, shnay loochot ha'breet, echad Elohaynoo she'bashamayim oova'aretz.

Who knows three? I know three: Three patriarchs, two tablets of the covenant.

One is our God who is in the heavens and the earth.

אַרְבַּע מִי יוֹדֵעַ? אַרְבַּע אֲנִי יוֹדֵעַ: אַרְבַּע אִמָּהוֹת, שְׁלֹשָׁה אָבוֹת, שְׁנֵי לֻחוֹת הַבְּרִית, אֶחָד אֱלֹהֵינוּ שֶׁבַּשָּׁמַיִם וּבָאָרֶץ.

Arba mee yodaya? Arba anee yodaya: Arba eemahot, shlosha avot, shnay loochot ha'breet, echad Elohaynoo she'bashamayim oova'aretz.

Who knows four? I know four: Four matriarchs, three patriarchs, two tablets of the covenant.

One is our God who is in the heavens and the earth.

חֲמִשָּׁה מִי יוֹדֵעַ? חֲמִשָּׁה אֲנִי יוֹדֵעַ: חֲמִשָּׁה חוּמְשֵׁי תוֹרָה, אַרְבַּע אִמָּהוֹת, שְׁלֹשָׁה אָבוֹת, שְׁנֵי לֻחוֹת הַבְּרִית, אֶחָד אֱלֹהֵינוּ שֶׁבַּשָּׁמַיִם וּבָאָרֶץ.

Chameesha mee yodaya? Chameesha anee yodaya: Chameesha choomshay Torah, arba eemahot, shlosha avot, shnay loochot ha'breet, echad Elohaynoo she'bashamayim oova'aretz.

Who knows five? I know five: Five books of the Torah, four matriarchs, three patriarchs, two tablets of the covenant.

One is our God who is in the heavens and the earth.

שִׁשָּׁה מִי יוֹדֵעַ? שִׁשָּׁה אֲנִי יוֹדֵעַ: שִׁשָּׁה סִדְרֵי מִשְׁנָה, חֲמִשָּׁה חוּמְשֵׁי תוֹרָה, אַרְבַּע אִמָּהוֹת, שְׁלֹשָׁה אָבוֹת, שְׁנֵי לֻחוֹת הַבְּרִית, אֶחָד אֱלֹהֵינוּ שֶׁבַּשָּׁמַיִם וּבָאָרֶץ.

Sheesha mee yodaya? Sheesha anee yodaya: Sheesha sidray Mishnah, chameesha choomshay Torah, arba eemahot, shlosha avot, shnay loochot ha'breet, echad Elohaynoo she'bashamayim oova'aretz.

Who knows six? I know six: Six orders of the Mishnah, five books of the Torah, four matriarchs, three patriarchs, two tablets of the covenant.

One is our God who is in the heavens and the earth.

שִׁבְעָה מִי יוֹדֵעַ? שִׁבְעָה אֲנִי יוֹדֵעַ: שִׁבְעָה יְמֵי שַׁבָּתָא, שִׁשָּׁה סִדְרֵי מִשְׁנָה, חֲמִשָּׁה חוּמְשֵׁי תוֹרָה, אַרְבַּע אִמָּהוֹת, שְׁלֹשָׁה אָבוֹת, שְׁנֵי לֻחוֹת הַבְּרִית, אֶחָד אֱלֹהֵינוּ שֶׁבַּשָּׁמַיִם וּבָאָרֶץ.

Shiv'a mee yodaya? Shiv'a anee yodaya: Shiv'a yemay Shabbata, sheesha sidray Mishnah, chameesha choomshay Torah, arba eemahot, shlosha avot, shnay loochot ha'breet, echad Elohaynoo she'bashamayim oova'aretz.

Who knows seven? I know seven: Seven days 'til the Sabbath, six orders of the Mishnah, five books of the Torah, four matriarchs, three patriarchs, two tablets of the covenant.

One is our God who is in the heavens and the earth.

שְׁמוֹנָה מִי יוֹדֵעַ? שְׁמוֹנָה אֲנִי יוֹדֵעַ: שְׁמוֹנָה יְמֵי מִילָה, שִׁבְעָה יְמֵי שַׁבַּתָּא, שִׁשָּׁה סִדְרֵי מִשְׁנָה, חֲמִשָּׁה חוּמְשֵׁי תוֹרָה, אַרְבַּע אִמָּהוֹת, שְׁלֹשָׁה אָבוֹת, שְׁנֵי לֻחוֹת הַבְּרִית, אֶחָד אֱלֹהֵינוּ שֶׁבַּשָּׁמַיִם וּבָאָרֶץ.

Shmona mee yodaya? Shmona anee yodaya: Shmona yemay meela, shiv'a yemay Shabbata, sheesha sidray Mishnah, chameesha choomshay Torah, arba eemahot, shlosha avot, shnay loochot ha'breet, echad Elohaynoo she'bashamayim oova'aretz.

Who knows eight? I know eight: Eight days 'til the brit milah, seven days 'til the Sabbath, six orders of the Mishnah, five books of the Torah, four matriarchs, three patriarchs, two tablets of the covenant.

One is our God who is in the heavens and the earth.

תִּשְׁעָה מִי יוֹדֵעַ? תִּשְׁעָה אֲנִי יוֹדֵעַ: תִּשְׁעָה יַרְחֵי לֵדָה, שְׁמוֹנָה יְמֵי מִילָה, שִׁבְעָה יְמֵי שַׁבַּתָּא, שִׁשָּׁה סִדְרֵי מִשְׁנָה, חֲמִשָּׁה חוּמְשֵׁי תוֹרָה, אַרְבַּע אִמָּהוֹת, שְׁלֹשָׁה אָבוֹת, שְׁנֵי לֻחוֹת הַבְּרִית, אֶחָד אֱלֹהֵינוּ שֶׁבַּשָּׁמַיִם וּבָאָרֶץ.

Tish'a mee yodaya? Tish'a anee yodaya: Tish'a yarchay layda, shmona yemay meela, shiv'a yemay Shabbata, sheesha sidray Mishnah, chameesha choomshay Torah, arba eemahot, shlosha avot, shnay loochot ha'breet, echad Elohaynoo she'bashamayim oova'aretz.

Who knows nine? I know nine: Nine months for birth, eight days 'til the brit milah, seven days 'til the Sabbath, six orders of the Mishnah, five books of the Torah, four matriarchs, three patriarchs, two tablets of the covenant.

One is our God who is in the heavens and the earth.

עֲשָׂרָה מִי יוֹדֵעַ? עֲשָׂרָה אֲנִי יוֹדֵעַ: עֲשָׂרָה דִבְּרַיָּא, תִּשְׁעָה יַרְחֵי לֵדָה, שְׁמוֹנָה יְמֵי מִילָה, שִׁבְעָה יְמֵי שַׁבַּתָּא, שִׁשָּׁה סִדְרֵי מִשְׁנָה, חֲמִשָּׁה חוּמְשֵׁי תוֹרָה, אַרְבַּע אִמָּהוֹת, שְׁלֹשָׁה אָבוֹת, שְׁנֵי לֻחוֹת הַבְּרִית, אֶחָד אֱלֹהֵינוּ שֶׁבַּשָּׁמַיִם וּבָאָרֶץ.

Asara mee yodaya? Asara anee yodaya: Asarah dib'rai'ya, tish'a yarchay layda, shmona yemay meela, shiv'a yemay Shabbata, sheesha sidray Mishnah, chameesha choomshay Torah, arba eemahot, shlosha avot, shnay loochot ha'breet, echad Elohaynoo she'bashamayim oova'aretz.

Who knows ten? I know ten: Ten utterances, nine months for birth, eight days 'til the brit milah, seven days 'til the Sabbath, six orders of the Mishnah, five books of the Torah, four matriarchs, three patriarchs, two tablets of the covenant.

One is our God who is in the heavens and the earth.

אַחַד עָשָׂר מִי יוֹדֵעַ? אַחַד עָשָׂר אֲנִי יוֹדֵעַ: אַחַד עָשָׂר כּוֹכְבַיָּא, עֲשָׂרָה דִבְּרַיָּא, תִּשְׁעָה יַרְחֵי לֵדָה, שְׁמוֹנָה יְמֵי מִילָה, שִׁבְעָה יְמֵי שַׁבַּתָּא, שִׁשָּׁה סִדְרֵי מִשְׁנָה, חֲמִשָּׁה חוּמְשֵׁי תוֹרָה, אַרְבַּע אִמָּהוֹת, שְׁלֹשָׁה אָבוֹת, שְׁנֵי לֻחוֹת הַבְּרִית, אֶחָד אֱלֹהֵינוּ שֶׁבַּשָּׁמַיִם וּבָאָרֶץ.

Achad asar mee yodaya? Achad asar anee yodaya: Achad asar koch'vai'ya, asarah dib'rai'ya, tish'a yarchay layda, shmona yemay meela, shiv'a yemay Shabbata, sheesha sidray Mishnah, chameesha choomshay Torah, arba eemahot, shlosha avot, shnay loochot ha'breet, echad Elohaynoo she'bashamayim oova'aretz.

Why Jack Black Is Obsessed with "Chad Gadya"

As we mentioned earlier, some of the best rock songs cover heavy subjects masked by lighthearted melodies, and that's how **"Chad Gadya"** rolls. A meditation on the cycle of life set to a chirpy tune, it starts out with a dad buying his child an adorable little goat and ends with the Almighty killing the Angel of Death. Wow! It's no wonder that rock musician/actor/comic Jack Black counts it among his favorites. "I actually do love that song," he says. "It's kind of like the original heavy metal song. I remember when I was a kid I was obsessed with the Angel of Death; it was very Black Sabbath."

Black has another reason to appreciate Passover—it was at a Seder that he discovered acting at age eight. The hostess, a family friend, organized a post-dinner round of Freeze, the classic game used in improv comedy. "I couldn't stand being in the audience," he says. "I had to be on the living room stage."

Jack Black has recorded "Chad Gadya," and he says he performed it for administrators at a Hebrew school that he wanted his kids to attend.

Who knows eleven? I know eleven: Eleven stars, ten utterances, nine months for birth, eight days 'til the brit milah, seven days 'til the Sabbath, six orders of the Mishnah, five books of the Torah, four matriarchs, three patriarchs, two tablets of the covenant.

One is our God who is in the heavens and the earth.

שְׁנֵים עָשָׂר מִי יוֹדֵעַ? שְׁנֵים עָשָׂר אֲנִי יוֹדֵעַ: שְׁנֵים עָשָׂר שִׁבְטַיָּא, אַחַד עָשָׂר כּוֹכְבַיָּא, עֲשָׂרָה דִבְּרַיָּא, תִּשְׁעָה יַרְחֵי לֵדָה, שְׁמוֹנָה יְמֵי מִילָה, שִׁבְעָה יְמֵי שַׁבָּתָא, שִׁשָּׁה סִדְרֵי מִשְׁנָה, חֲמִשָּׁה חוּמְשֵׁי תוֹרָה, אַרְבַּע אִמָּהוֹת, שְׁלֹשָׁה אָבוֹת, שְׁנֵי לֻחוֹת הַבְּרִית, אֶחָד אֱלֹהֵינוּ שֶׁבַּשָּׁמַיִם וּבָאָרֶץ.

Shnaym asar mee yodaya? Shnaym asar anee yodaya: Shnaym asar shivtai'ya, achad asar koch'vai'ya, asarah dib'rai'ya, tish'a yarchay layda, shmona yemay meela, shiv'a yemay Shabbata, sheesha sidray Mishnah, chameesha choomshay Torah, arba eemahot, shlosha avot, shnay loochot ha'breet, echad Elohaynoo she'bashamayim oova'aretz.

Who knows twelve? I know twelve: Twelve tribes, eleven stars, ten utterances, nine months for birth, eight days 'til the brit milah, seven days 'til the Sabbath, six orders of the Mishnah, five books of the Torah, four matriarchs, three patriarchs, two tablets of the covenant.

One is our God who is in the heavens and the earth.

שְׁלֹשָׁה עָשָׂר מִי יוֹדֵעַ? שְׁלֹשָׁה עָשָׂר אֲנִי יוֹדֵעַ: שְׁלֹשָׁה עָשָׂר מִדַּיָּא. שְׁנֵים עָשָׂר שִׁבְטַיָּא, אַחַד עָשָׂר כּוֹכְבַיָּא, עֲשָׂרָה דִבְּרַיָּא, תִּשְׁעָה יַרְחֵי לֵדָה, שְׁמוֹנָה יְמֵי מִילָה, שִׁבְעָה יְמֵי שַׁבָּתָא, שִׁשָּׁה סִדְרֵי מִשְׁנָה, חֲמִשָּׁה חוּמְשֵׁי תוֹרָה, אַרְבַּע אִמָּהוֹת, שְׁלֹשָׁה אָבוֹת, שְׁנֵי לֻחוֹת הַבְּרִית, אֶחָד אֱלֹהֵינוּ שֶׁבַּשָּׁמַיִם וּבָאָרֶץ.

Shlosha asar mee yodaya? Shlosha asar anee yodaya: Shlosha asar mee'dai'ya, shnaym asar shivtai'ya, achad asar koch'vai'ya, asarah dib'rai'ya, tish'a yarchay layda, shmona yemay meela, shiv'a yemay Shabbata, sheesha sidray Mishnah, chameesha choomshay Torah, arba eemahot, shlosha avot, shnay loochot ha'breet, echad Elohaynoo she'bashamayim oova'aretz.

Who knows thirteen? I know thirteen: Thirteen attributes, twelve tribes, eleven stars, ten utterances, nine months for birth, eight days 'til the brit milah, seven days 'til the Sabbath, six orders of the Mishnah, five books of the Torah, four matriarchs, three patriarchs, two tablets of the covenant.

One is our God who is in the heavens and the earth.

"Chad Gadya" "חַד גַּדְיָא"
"One Little Goat"

חַד גַּדְיָא, חַד גַּדְיָא דְּזַבִּין אַבָּא בִּתְרֵי זוּזֵי, חַד גַּדְיָא, חַד גַּדְיָא.

Chad gadya, chad gadya. De'zabin aba bizray zoozay, chad gadya, chad gadya.

One goat, one goat that my father bought for two zuzim. One little goat, one little goat.

וְאָתָא שׁוּנְרָא וְאָכְלָה לְגַדְיָא, דְּזַבִּין אַבָּא בִּתְרֵי זוּזֵי. חַד גַּדְיָא, חַד גַּדְיָא.

V'asa shoonra ve'achla le'gadya, de'zabin aba bizray zoozay, chad gadya, chad gadya.

The cat came and ate the goat that my father bought for two zuzim. One little goat, one little goat.

וְאָתָא כַלְבָּא וְנָשַׁךְ לְשׁוּנְרָא, דְּאָכְלָה לְגַדְיָא, דְּזַבִּין אַבָּא בִּתְרֵי זוּזֵי. חַד גַּדְיָא, חַד גַּדְיָא.

V'asa kalba ve'nashach le'shoonra de'achla le'gadya, de'zabin aba bizray zoozay, chad gadya, chad gadya.

The dog came and bit the cat that ate the goat that my father bought for two zuzim. One little goat, one little goat.

וְאָתָא חוּטְרָא וְהִכָּה לְכַלְבָּא, דְּנָשַׁךְ לְשׁוּנְרָא, דְּאָכְלָה לְגַדְיָא, דְּזַבִּין אַבָּא בִּתְרֵי זוּזֵי. חַד גַּדְיָא, חַד גַּדְיָא.

V'asa chootra ve'heekah le'chalbah, de'nashach le'shoonra de'achla

le'gadya, de'zabin aba bizray zoozay, chad gadya, chad gadya.

The stick came and struck the dog that bit the cat that ate the goat that my father bought for two zuzim. One little goat, one little goat.

וְאָתָא נוּרָא וְשָׂרַף לְחוּטְרָא, דְּהִכָּה לְכַלְבָּא, דְּנָשַׁךְ לְשׁוּנְרָא, דְּאָכְלָה לְגַדְיָא, דְּזַבִּין אַבָּא בִּתְרֵי זוּזֵי. חַד גַּדְיָא, חַד גַּדְיָא.

V'asa noora ve'saraf le'chootra, de'heekah le'chalbah, de'nashach le'shoonra de'achla le'gadya, de'zabin aba bizray zoozay, chad gadya, chad gadya.

The fire came and burned the stick that hit the dog that bit the cat that ate the goat that my father bought for two zuzim. One little goat, one little goat.

וְאָתָא מַיָּא וְכָבָה לְנוּרָא, דְּשָׂרַף לְחוּטְרָא, דְּהִכָּה לְכַלְבָּא, דְּנָשַׁךְ לְשׁוּנְרָא, דְּאָכְלָה לְגַדְיָא, דְּזַבִּין אַבָּא בִּתְרֵי זוּזֵי. חַד גַּדְיָא, חַד גַּדְיָא.

V'asa mai'ya ve'chava le'noora de'saraf le'chootra, de'heekah le'chalbah, de'nashach le'shoonra de'achla le'gadya, de'zabin aba bizray zoozay, chad gadya, chad gadya.

The water came and put out the fire that burned the stick that hit the dog that bit the cat that ate the goat that my father bought for two zuzim. One little goat, one little goat.

"Blood of the Lamb" and Woody Guthrie's Jewish Fam

Though its title relates to the Passover story, Woody Guthrie's "Blood of the Lamb" was based on a classic nineteenth-century hymn by Evangelical Reverend Elisha A. Hoffman called **"Are You Washed in the Blood?"** It wasn't quite a song, either, just lyrics written down with thousands of others that the vastly prolific Guthrie never got around to recording.

Billy Bragg and Wilco set it to music on their collaboration *Mermaid Avenue Vol. II*, the second album on which they mined the Guthrie archives for his undiscovered lyrics. The album title is a tribute to the Coney Island, New York, block where the iconic folk troubadour lived with second wife, Marjorie Greenblatt, a Martha Graham dancer, and their children in the 1940s.

An Okie by birth, Guthrie wasn't Jewish. But Greenblatt and their kids, including singer Arlo and Guthrie Foundation head Nora—who opened the archives to Bragg and Wilco—were. Greenblatt's mother, Aliza Greenblatt, was a renowned Yiddish poet and activist who lived a couple of blocks away from the Guthries in Coney Island, home to a thriving, artsy Jewish community at the time. His mother-in-law had a big influence on Guthrie, whose work included Hanukkah songs and other Jewish themes. Nora and Arlo's Bubbe Aliza sang to them in Yiddish and cooked traditional eastern European–inspired foods for them. When Arlo reached bar mitzvah age, his folks contacted the Rabbinical School at Yeshiva University to find a tutor; the student they sent was Meir Kahane, future cofounder of the Jewish Defense League.

The 1930s Dust Bowl that turned Guthrie into a migrant had put him on a path that led to New York City, where he wrote his most well-known song, **"This Land Is Your Land,"** as well as a lifelong quest for social justice. During World War II, Guthrie wrote the song **"Talking Hitler's Head Off Blues"** and scrawled the words "This Machine Kills Fascists" on his guitar. For American Jewish immigrants with a history of expulsion or murder at the hands of pharaohs, kings, tsars, and other autocrats, this philosophy aligned.

Near the end of his life, Guthrie was visited by another poetic midwestern songwriter with a keen grasp of the mythology of fame—Bob Dylan. Guthrie mentored the young Jewish bard, but his impact on rock 'n' roll extends far beyond. From Jeff Tweedy and Billy Bragg to Bruce Springsteen and Rage Against the Machine to the Clash and Johnny Cash, Guthrie's Americana-Dust-Bowl-meets-New-York-melting-pot aesthetic gave rock music both empathy and righteous indignation.

אָתָא תוֹרָא וְשָׁתָה לְמַיָּא, דְּכָבָה לְנוּרָא, דְּשָׂרַף
לְחוּטְרָא, דְּהִכָּה לְכַלְבָּא, דְּנָשַׁךְ לְשׁוּנְרָא, דְּאָכְלָה
לְגַדְיָא, דְּזַבִּין אַבָּא בִּתְרֵי זוּזֵי. חַד גַּדְיָא, חַד גַּדְיָא.

V'asa toorah ve'shata le' mai'ya de'chava le'noora de'saraf le'chootra, de'heekah le'chalbah, de'nashach le'shoonra de'achla le'gadya, de'zabin aba bizray zoozay, chad gadya, chad gadya.

The bull came and drank the water that put out the fire that burned the stick that hit the dog that bit the cat that ate the goat that my father bought for two zuzim. One little goat, one little goat.

וְאָתָא הַשּׁוֹחֵט וְשָׁחַט לְתוֹרָא, דְּשָׁתָה לְמַיָּא, דְּכָבָה
לְנוּרָא, דְּשָׂרַף לְחוּטְרָא, דְּהִכָּה לְכַלְבָּא, דְּנָשַׁךְ
לְשׁוּנְרָא, דְּאָכְלָה לְגַדְיָא, דְּזַבִּין אַבָּא בִּתְרֵי זוּזֵי. חַד
גַּדְיָא, חַד גַּדְיָא.

V'asa ha'shochayt ve'shachat le'toorah de'shata le' mai'ya de'chava le'noora de'saraf le'chootra, de'heekah le'chalbah, de'nashach le'shoonra de'achla le'gadya, de'zabin aba bizray zoozay, chad gadya, chad gadya.

The shochet* came and slaughtered the bull that drank the water that put out the fire that burned the stick that hit the dog that bit the cat that ate the goat that my father bought for two zuzim. One little goat, one little goat.

וְאָתָא מַלְאַךְ הַמָּוֶת וְשָׁחַט לְשׁוֹחֵט, דְּשָׁחַט
לְתוֹרָא, דְּשָׁתָה לְמַיָּא, דְּכָבָה לְנוּרָא, דְּשָׂרַף
לְחוּטְרָא, דְּהִכָּה לְכַלְבָּא, דְּנָשַׁךְ לְשׁוּנְרָא, דְּאָכְלָה
לְגַדְיָא, דְּזַבִּין אַבָּא בִּתְרֵי זוּזֵי. חַד גַּדְיָא, חַד גַּדְיָא.

V'asa malach ha'mavet ve'shachat la'shochayt, de'shachat le'toorah de'shata le'mai'ya de'chava le'noora de'saraf le'chootra, de'heekah le'chalbah, de'nashach le'shoonra de'achla le'gadya, de'zabin aba bizray zoozay, chad gadya, chad gadya.

The Angel of Death came and slaughtered the shochet who slaughtered the bull that drank the water that put out the fire that burned the stick that hit the dog that bit the cat that ate the goat that my father bought for two zuzim. One little goat, one little goat.

וְאָתָא הַקָּדוֹשׁ בָּרוּךְ הוּא וְשָׁחַט לְמַלְאַךְ הַמָּוֶת,
דְּשָׁחַט לְשׁוֹחֵט, דְּשָׁחַט לְתוֹרָא, דְּשָׁתָה לְמַיָּא,
דְּכָבָה לְנוּרָא, דְּשָׂרַף לְחוּטְרָא, דְּהִכָּה לְכַלְבָּא,
דְּנָשַׁךְ לְשׁוּנְרָא, דְּאָכְלָה לְגַדְיָא, דְּזַבִּין אַבָּא בִּתְרֵי
זוּזֵי. חַד גַּדְיָא, חַד גַּדְיָא.

V'asa hakodesh baruch hoo ve'shachat le'malach ha'mavet, de'shachat le'shochayt, de'shachat le'toorah, de'shata le'mai'ya, de'chava le'noora, de'saraf le'chootra, de'heekah le'chalbah, de'nashach le'shoonra, de'achla le'gadya, de'zabin aba bizray zoozay, chad gadya, chad gadya.

Then the Holy One, blessed be, came and slaughtered the Angel of Death who slaughtered the shochet who slaughtered the bull that drank the water that put out the fire that burned the stick that hit the dog that bit the cat that ate the goat that my father bought for two zuzim. One little goat, one little goat.

---

* A shochet is a kosher slaughterer.

Games and Trivia

Passover "AD LIB"

The Pharaoh known as Ramses II was having a (adjective)_____ day. His adopted grandson, the Israelite Moses, showed up at the palace with a big ask:

Moses said, "Let My (noun)_____ Go."

Pharaoh feared the Israelites would (verb)_____. So, he put on his (noun)_____ and climbed into his chariot to survey his (noun)_____. He did not notice anything (adjective)_____.

Pharaoh decided to return to his palace. He was hungry, so he had his servant prepare a (animal)_____ feast. After dining he let out a loud (sound)_____. The whole palace shook like a (adjective)_____ earthquake.

The (adjective)_____ Pharaoh decided to take a nap. He snored like a (adjective)_____ (animal)_____. His sphynx cats ran for cover. He (verb, past tense)_____ in his bed. He dreamed that all his (adjective)_____ wives ran away. While tossing and turning, he rolled on a (noun)_____ and (verb, past tense)_____.

The moral of the story: Never sleep next to a (adjective)_____ Pharaoh!

Passover Trivia:

More Than Four Questions

What kind of bread are Jews commanded to eat during the Passover Seder to commemorate their escape from Egypt?

A. multigrain **B.** gluten-free **C.** unbuttered **D.** unleavened

(*Hint: We tossed the loaves of bread on our backs and booked into the desert under the hot sun.*)

Which Jewish OG son of a patriarch was the first Israelite to rise to power in Egypt?

A. Abraham **B.** Isaac **C.** Jacob **D.** Joseph

(*Hint: He was the only OG with an Amazing Technicolor Dreamcoat.*)

What river was Moses floated in as a baby?

A. the Nile **B.** the Rashid **C.** the Euphrates **D.** the Sinai

(*Hint: Moses's mom, Yocheved, was in "denial" of Pharaoh's order to kill Jewish baby boys.*)

Who were the siblings of Moses?

A. Ramses and Bithiah **B.** Aaron and Miriam **C.** Jacob and Esau
D. Jethro and Myrtle

(*Hint: His name sounds exactly like Elvis's middle name.*)

What did the Israelites build in the desert that made Moses really, really angry?

A. $100,000 Pyramid **B.** Wheel of Fortune **C.** Golden Calf
D. Bronze-Age Bear

(*Hint: Moses hurled the Ten Commandments when he saw this glittering little heifer.*)

God sends which of these bands to Egypt to unleash fury?

A. Band of Susans **B.** Band of Evil Angels **C.** the Mummies **D.** Yo La Tengo

(*Hint: They're not actually a band, but they are God's emissaries.*)

What is the meaning of "Dayenu"?

A. It Would Have Been Enough **B.** It's Never Enough **C.** Enough Is Enough
D. Tears Are Not Enough

(*Hint: Just a miracle or two would do.*)

Which of these foods is *not* traditionally consumed on Passover?

A. chicken **B.** gefilte fish **C.** donuts **D.** eggs

(*Hint: We eat this treat on Hanukkah to commemorate a day's worth of oil lasting for eight days.*)

Bonus Round for Phish Phans

Here's a handy chart to help you debate the merits of gefilte fish versus the band Phish, along with a trivia question: **Name a Phish song that contains the word "lumpy."**

Gefilte fish vs. the band Phish		
White + Lumpy	✓	✓
Salty + sweet	✓	✓
Jellied	✓	
Jammed		✓
Devoted Cult following	✓	✓
Headliner		✓
Inspired podcasts	✓	✓
Catholic origins	✓	

The answer: "Carini"

The *Rock 'n' Roll Haggadah* Playlist

CONGRATULATIONS ON MAKING IT THROUGH A SEDER!

Whether you're the host or a guest, it's considered a mitzvah to participate. We've created this Passover-themed playlist for you to enjoy anytime, pre- or post–festive meal. It may be found under "Rock 'n' Roll Haggadah" on Spotify. Make it an after-dinner dance party if you like or plotz ("collapse or faint") if you prefer, but you'd better move fast if you want to land a coveted spot on the sofa.

KISS, "God Gave Rock and Roll to You II"

The Jam, "Absolute Beginners"

Funkadelic, "One Nation Under a Groove"

The Hollies, "King Midas in Reverse"

Billy Preston, "The Same Thing Again"

Avril Lavigne, "It's Complicated"

Led Zeppelin, "Houses of the Holy"

Bob Dylan, "The Times They Are A-Changin'"

Fun, "We Are Young"

Fun, "Carry On"

John Lennon, "Meat City"

Emmylou Harris,
"Two More Bottles of Wine"

Robert Earl Keen,
"Farm Fresh Onions"

Ed Sheeran, "Salt Water"

Led Zeppelin, "The Ocean"

Smokey Robinson & the Miracles,
"Tracks of My Tears"

The Gourds, "Gangsta Lean"

Bill Withers, "Lean on Me"

Scandal, "Goodbye to You"

ZZ Top,
"Beer Drinkers & Hell Raisers"

Tom Jones, "It's Not Unusual"

Cracker, "Low"

Steely Dan, "Everything Must Go"

The Stooges, "Search and Destroy"

Parliament, "Flashlight"

Waylon Jennings, "Small Packages"

Kings of Leon, "Pyro"

Jimmy Spicer,
"Money (Dollar Bill Y'all)"

Cheap Trick, "The Flame"

New Order, "Temptation"

The Proclaimers,
"I'm Gonna Be (500 Miles)"

Bruce Springsteen, "Hungry Heart"

Low Cut Connie, "King of the Jews"

Desmond Dekker, "Israelites"

Anthrax, "I'm the Man"

Phish, "Yerushalayim Shel Zahav"

Louis Armstrong, "Russian Lullaby"

Jackson Browne,
"Running on Empty"

Slim Gaillard, "Matzoh Balls"

Billy Squier, "In the Dark"

INXS, "Bitter Tears"

The Jam, "Bricks and Mortar"

UB40, "Red Red Wine"

Neil Diamond, "Red Red Wine"

Roger Miller, "Chug-A-Lug"

Blind Melon,
"Three Is a Magic Number"

The Crows with Melino & His
Orchestra, "Mambo Shevitz
(Man O Man)"

The Supremes,
"You Keep Me Hangin' On"

Leonard Cohen, "Born in Chains"

The Doobie Brothers,
"Rockin' Down the Highway"

Jackie Wilson, "Lonely Teardrops"

Roy Orbison, "Crying"

The Bangles, "Walk Like an Egyptian"

Marvin Gaye, "What's Going On"

The Flaming Lips, "Do You Realize??"

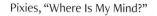

Pixies, "Where Is My Mind?"

Elvis Costello & the Attractions (or Nick Lowe), "(What's So Funny 'Bout) Peace, Love and Understanding"

Slash's Snakepit, "Ain't Life Grand"

Heart, "Magic Man"

Tom Petty and the Heartbreakers, "Don't Do Me Like That"

Cheap Trick, "The Dream Police"

Nirvana, "All Apologies"

Imagine Dragons, "Bones"

Madonna, "Holiday"

The Police, "King of Pain"

Coldplay, "A Sky Full of Stars"

Fear Factory, "New Messiah"

Sweet, "Action"

The Bongos, "The Bulrushes"

Nick Gilder, "Hot Child in the City"

Al Green, "Take Me to the River"

Nick Cave and the Bad Seeds, "The Weeping Song"

Oasis, "Wonderwall"

OutKast, "Hey Ya!"

Alanis Morissette, "You Learn"

Bruce Springsteen, "Born to Run"

Blue Öyster Cult, "Burnin' for You"

Radiohead, "Burning Bush"

Taylor Swift, "Holy Ground"

Bruce Springsteen, "Prove It All Night"

Alanis Morissette, "Hand in My Pocket"

Bon Jovi, "Blood in the Water"

Earl King, "Trick Bag"

Billie Eilish, "You Should See Me in a Crown"

Aretha Franklin, "Chain of Fools"

Tears for Fears, "Everybody Wants to Rule the World"

Collective Soul, "Shine"

Angel, "White Hot"

The Rascals, "People Got to Be Free"

Tom Petty and the Heartbreakers, "I Won't Back Down"

Hoagy Carmichael, "Lazy Bones"

Def Leppard, "Promises"

Dire Straits, "Brothers in Arms"

ELO, "Strange Magic"

Five Man Electrical Band, "Signs"

Lenny Kravitz, "Are You Gonna Go My Way?"

Matthew Sweet, "Divine Intervention"

CHVRCHES, "Strong Hand"

Eric Burdon and War, "Spill the Wine"

Taylor Swift, "Bad Blood"

Lou Reed (feat. David Bowie), "Hop Frog"

Pearl Jam, "Bugs"

The Rolling Stones, "Beast of Burden"

Foo Fighters, "For All the Cows"

The Youngbloods, "Darkness, Darkness"

Lou Reed, "Ocean"

Bruce Springsteen, "O Mary Don't You Weep"

George Harrison, "Between the Devil & the Deep Blue Sea"

Bob Marley & the Wailers, "Exodus"

The Flower Kings, "Sword of God"

Creedence Clearwater Revival, "Bad Moon Rising"

Metallica, "Creeping Death"

Genesis, "Throwing It All Away"

Journey, "Any Way You Want It"

Drake, "Hotline Bling"

ELO, "Telephone Line"

Phoebe Bridgers, "Smoke Signals"

Stevie Wonder, "Higher Ground"

Band of Heathens, "Golden Calf"

Twisted Sister, "We're Not Gonna Take It"

Mötley Crüe, "Don't Go Away Mad (Just Go Away)"

Thin Lizzy, "Get Out of Here"

The Weeknd, "False Idols"

Morphine, "Gone for Good"

Disturbed, "A Reason to Fight"

Uncle Tupelo, "Effigy"

The Libertines, "Over It Again"

The Beatles, "We Can Work It Out"

Bruce Springsteen, "The Promised Land"

Bob Dylan, "Little Moses"

Louis Armstrong, "Shadrack"

The Grateful Dead, "Uncle John's Band"

Leonard Cohen, "After the Sabbath Prayers"

Taylor Swift, "The Best Day"

Queen, "Bohemian Rhapsody"

Jane's Addiction, "Been Caught Stealing"

Bo Diddley, "Before You Accuse Me"

Derek and the Dominos, "Layla"

Johnny Cash, "The Ten Commandments"

Jerry Garcia Band, "Waiting for a Miracle"

The Grateful Dead, "Promised Land"

Jerry Garcia Band, "Ain't No Bread in the Breadbox"

Louis Armstrong, "Go Down Moses"

Kris Kristofferson (or Janis Joplin), "Me and Bobby McGee"

Booker T. & the M.G.s, "Green Onions"

Cake, "The Distance"

DEVO, "Whip It Good"

Dazz Band, "Let It Whip"

Johnny Thunders & the Heartbreakers, "It's Not Enough"

Leonard Cohen, "Anthem"

Aretha Franklin, "Respect"

The Incredible String Band, "The Water Song"

The Go-Go's, "Our Lips Are Sealed"

Kosha Dillz, Hila the Killa, "Big Matzah"

The Jam, "The Bitterest Pill"

Three Days Grace, "Pain"

Freak Nasty, "Da' Dip"

Carole King, "Bitter with the Sweet"

Sam and Dave, "Wrap It Up"

Warren Zevon, "I'll Sleep When I'm Dead"

Joan Jett and the Blackhearts, "Hide and Seek"

ABBA, "The Winner Takes It All"

The Dave Clark Five, "Bits and Pieces"

J.J. Cale, "After Midnight"

Joe Walsh, "All Night Long"

Sam and Dave, "I Thank You"

Simon & Garfunkel, "The Sound of Silence"

Laura Nyro, "Eli's Coming"

Chumbawamba, "Tubthumper"

Billy Bragg and Wilco, "Blood of the Lamb"

Iris DeMent, "Let the Mystery Be"

Woody Guthrie, "This Land Is Your Land"

Leonard Cohen, "Hallelujah"

Elvis Presley (or Tom Jones), "Green, Green Grass of Home"

Acknowledgments

Thank you:

Samantha Weiner

Gina Navaroli

Lenny Kaye

Joan Brookbank

Rabbi Molly Karp

Carly Sommerstein

Rima Weinberg

Lawrence Ochs

Ron Metz

Rob Santos

Cary Baker

Peter Himmelman

Jessica Linker

Spencer Tweedy

Michael Rosenblatt

Rami Jaffee

Jon Weiswasser

Bob Gruen

Carol Klefner

Jeannette Ferber

Michael Dorf and City Winery

Sabrina Teitelbaum

Adam Weiner

Jill Sternheimer

Lynnea Villanova and Andrei Codrescu

Andrew and Julia Gottesman

Doreen Cronin

Jay, Abby, Eleanor Beth, and David Gottesman

Beth El Synagogue Center, New Rochelle, NY: Rabbi David Schuck, Rabbi

Zachary Sitkin, Cantor Gaby Schvartz, and Zoe Raynes

Susanna Levin

Jennifer Cohan

Shirley Halperin

Mitch Myers

Rabbi Margie Slome

Suzanne Glickman

Mary Ellen Doyle

Holly Aguirre

Adam Budofsky

Jack Grace

Janet Rosen

Mike Greenhaus and Relix

Sami Rosnov

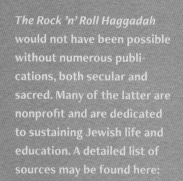

The Rock 'n' Roll Haggadah would not have been possible without numerous publications, both secular and sacred. Many of the latter are nonprofit and are dedicated to sustaining Jewish life and education. A detailed list of sources may be found here:

BOOM BAM